SIMPLY DYN[AMIC]

SAMPLER QUILTS

Marianne L. Hatton

American Quilter's Society
P. O. Box 3290 • Paducah, KY 42002-3290
www.AmericanQuilter.com

Located in Paducah, Kentucky, the American Quilter's Society (AQS) is dedicated to promoting the accomplishments of today's quilters. Through its publications and events, AQS strives to honor today's quiltmakers and their work and to inspire future creativity and innovation in quiltmaking.

EXECUTIVE BOOK EDITOR: ANDI MILAM REYNOLDS
SENIOR BOOK EDITOR: LINDA BAXTER LASCO
GRAPHIC DESIGN: ELAINE WILSON
COVER DESIGN: MICHAEL BUCKINGHAM
QUILT PHOTOGRAPHY: CHARLES R. LYNCH
HOW-TO PHOTOGRAPHY: MARIANNE L. HATTON

Additional copies of this book may be ordered from the American Quilter's Society, PO Box 3290, Paducah, KY 42002-3290, or online at www.AmericanQuilter.com.

Library of Congress Cataloging-in-Publication Data

Hatton, Marianne L.
  Simply dynamic sampler quilts / by Marianne L. Hatton.
    p. cm.
  ISBN 978-1-57432-670-3
  1. Patchwork--Patterns. 2. Quilting--Patterns. I. Title.
  TT835H3437 2010
  746.46--dc22
                            2010019770

COVER: MY GARDEN, *detail. Full quilt page 21.*
TITLE PAGE: COOL AND SHADY, *detail. Full quilt page 32.*
RIGHT: ITALIAN MOSAIC, *detail. Full quilt page 19.*

Proudly printed and bound in the
United States of America

Dedication

This book is dedicated to the memory of my late parents, Janet and Vic Lawrence, who were there at the beginning but not at the finish. For my father, who so enjoyed what he did see of the book, and for my mother especially, whom I taught to quilt, but who, more importantly, first taught me to sew.

Acknowledgments

The writing of this book would have been much less enjoyable were it not for the caring, encouragement, and support of so many people. Thank you to all of my dear friends and family who urged me gently forward and have listened patiently to my talking about the book for so long!

I am most grateful to all of my wonderful students who continue to inspire me, and to all of you who made sampler quilts. Thank you for allowing me access to your quilts for consideration and inclusion in the book, in particular to those of you whose quilts appear, be it whole, in part, or in spirit, for sharing them and allowing them to be away from you for many months!

Special thanks indeed to Sally Cameron, my first ever quilt student, for ITALIAN MOSAIC—what a gift you are! I am so grateful to Kristine Lundblad, Fran Sharp, and Carol Ballou for their most extraordinary gifts of time and incredible talent! Thank you also to Valerie Hearder and Sylvia Einstein for their valuable insight and affirmation that I was on the right track, and to Nancy Halpern for reinforcing my belief that "quilters need to get over their fear of templates"! My appreciation also to Jane Barnett and her lovely staff at Quilter's Way in Concord, Massachusetts, for their enthusiastic support always.

I am greatly indebted to those whose patterns grace the quilts, in particular Carol Doak, Margaret Rolfe, Mary Jo Hiney, Jodie Davis, and Linda Hampton Schiffer whose lovely FPP designs are sprinkled liberally throughout the quilts in the book.

My dear family—my sons Kent, for his computer wizardry, and Ross, who lends an excellent eye for color, and my husband, Alan, whose patience, goodwill, and sense of humor helped me meet deadlines and whose love and support enable me to do what I do best. Thank you.

I am so honored to have AQS publish my book. Thank you to Andi Reynolds for her confidence, gracious help, and support, and to Linda Lasco, my editor, for so beautifully transforming my manuscript into a book with enthusiasm and impeccable attention to detail, along with the design team of Elaine Wilson, Michael Buckingham, and Charles Lynch, who all worked their magic to bring it into being.

To each of you who has been there along the way, thank you from the bottom of my heart.

Marianne Hatton
SUDBURY, MASSACHUSETTS

OPPOSITE: BACKYARD BIRDS, *42" x 48". Made by Janet Lyons, Sudbury, MA.*

Contents

Causee and Doak credits page 94

foreword

The sampler quilt was, for a very long time, the classic choice for teaching new quilters a compendium of different techniques, allowing them to showcase their newly acquired skills in a single piece. There are probably hundreds of thousands of examples of these quilts in the world today, testimonies to patient teachers and to their students eager to master the basics of a newfound passion. There are also many that might qualify as master quilts, done by quilters with a great deal of experience, showing off beautifully their years of knowledge and skill.

I have always valued sampler quilts as a progressive tool for acquiring the skills needed to create virtually any type of quilt later on. Of late, however, I have noticed fewer samplers at quilt shows and started to wonder how they might again become a favored means of learning a comprehensive set of skills—one that would enable quilters to easily tackle any and all elements of quilting, and move confidently into exploring quilts of their own design.

The types of quilts proposed in this book may be rooted in tradition but they are firmly grounded in the present. They have moved a long way away from the classic sampler rendition of rows of like-sized blocks. The quilts incorporate some contemporary and unusual (for a sampler, that is) techniques into the mix. Choice of a theme adds an element of interest. They will have you thinking about design and creating something worthy of much more than a passing glance at a quilt show.

It is my goal that this book will help instill in you a sense of confidence in tackling elements of design and color right from the beginning. I intend it to be of use to quiltmakers setting off on their journey through the amazing world of quilting, be it solo or in a class setting, and hope that it may provide teachers with a ready guide for this type of quilt. I also hope it will be inspiring to those with significant experience, but who may never have worked on a quilt in this particular way before.

Many of these quilts are hung in prominent places in my students' homes. They are, indeed, lovely to look at and worthy of being shown. I love seeing the quilts again, long after class has ended, and am so proud of my students and my friends who worked really hard to master the processes required to bring the quilts to completion. My grateful thanks to each one of them, for it is because of their dedication to the task that this book comes alive with color and pattern.

Introduction

The premise of these "next generation" sampler quilts is to work with different-sized blocks, blending them into a cohesive, balanced whole that may even have a story to tell about you and your interests, loves, or passions! It is an opportunity for learning several techniques that even some long-time quiltmakers may never have tried and that are seldom used all together in one quilt.

I like to call these samplers composition quilts. I love watching my students compose their own quilts, gathering confidence and new skills along the way. I find the quilts work best when the fabrics chosen unify the quilts. They become even better with a common theme and some attention paid to some simple principles of design.

When you look closely, you may be surprised to find that all the quilts in this book, even the more pictorial ones, use the same set of techniques, yet with very different outcomes. This book provides many ideas of where to begin but it does not provide many patterns. Think of it as a launching pad. It will guide you along the way toward your own unique interpretation. You will be encouraged to find the freedom to be creative within a framework.

The quilt design will not be final before you begin stitching. The overall concept will be considered first. Thereafter, the design will happen as the construction of components progresses, allowing a flexible design to emerge. Some quilters will finalize their design and know exactly what each quilt will look like before they ever take a stitch. I have never been able to work in that way, preferring the mystery of the unexpected outcome, making design decisions as I go. I have constructed this book in the same way.

If you are open to and will enjoy a surprise ending, I strongly suggest you jump in with only a little of the planning in mind. Be open to some spontaneous decisions as you go forward. It works! Bring your color sensibility, your ideas for a theme, and your personal preferences.

The quilt will be finished when you decide it is big enough. There are no dimensions, no constraints, and no decisions that need be made on that score. It will contain as many pieces as you want it to have and truly be composed of mostly your own ideas.

I recommend reading through pages 8–33 before you begin so you have some sense of where the project is heading. If the processes are new to you, you will grow into each stage, gaining experience as you go. If some is repeat material for you, you will draw on your former training and expand on it.

What I love most about quiltmaking is the ability to make each quilt uniquely one's own. Your sampler quilt will be very different from others you may have made before, and it will be a testimony to your patience and accomplishment.

The Stages of Making Your Sampler Quilt: A Visual Progression

Start thinking about possibilities for a theme.

Choose a color scheme.

Start gathering fabrics. Buy some or pull from your collection.

Plunge in and start making a block. The Log Cabin block is a good place to start as it uses most of your fabrics right away.

Make a checkerboard border using two (or more) favorite fabrics.

Start to make a paper map—your GridMap, the master plan for your quilt.

See if you can find a few more fabrics. Selecting a border fabric sometimes helps to focus the project.

Start working on blocks with appliqué and curved seams.

As you make a block, add the scaled paper equivalent to your GridMap. Where it goes is not important at this stage, but it will start you thinking about your final arrangement while considering design principles such as visual weight and balance.

Add even more fabrics if you can. The more fabrics, the more interesting the quilt.

Try the fun of foundation paper piecing.

Keep adding scaled paper versions of your blocks to the GridMap, trying out different placement possibilities.

Try the most challenging piece of the project— the Kaleidoscope block. You are ready!

Start putting your completed blocks up on a design wall to "audition" different arrangements. Step back and enjoy the vertical approach.

When you have your major block components, assess what gaps need filling in and make small filler units.

LEFT: *The pieced strip to the left of the Flying Geese acts as a filler.*

Start piecing the blocks and fillers into larger components, then piece them together.

Make corner blocks to add to the theme and extend the interest out further.

Add the corners into the outer border.

Back it, baste it, quilt it, and bind it.

Make a label for the back. Your heirs should know who made it, when, and maybe even why.

Done! Take a bow.

Anatomy of a Quilt

A quilt is composed of three layers—a quilt **top**, a **backing**, and a layer of **batting** between the two. The top may be just a single layer of cloth, or it may be pieced together in a decorative design. It often has one or more borders. The back is a layer of cloth, similar to that used in the quilt top. The batting may be made of cotton, wool, polyester, silk, or a blend of these and other fibers.

The three layers are held together by stitching—quilting—which also can serve as a decorative element. The quilting may be done by hand or machine.

The binding secures and neatens the edges of the three layers and adds a small but important decorative finish, rather like a very narrow picture frame.

This diagram illustrates the concept of a next generation sampler quilt and shows the different techniques and elements.

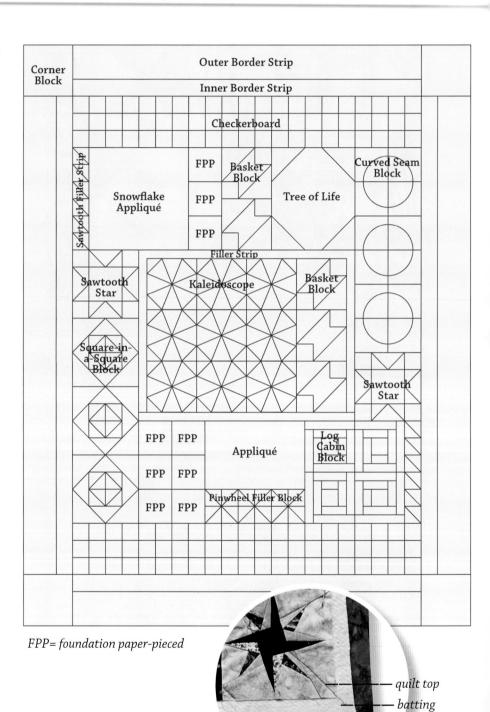

FPP= foundation paper-pieced

— quilt top
— batting
— backing

Design Considerations and Tactics

Take a step into the design arena. Yes you can!

Let's talk about themes and color schemes and a few other things to be thinking about that are relevant to your quilt.

Choosing a Theme

Well, if not choosing a theme, then at least thinking about one! If some of the motifs and blocks you choose have a pictorial element to them, they will help impart a theme to your quilt. A theme can guide your choice of a color scheme and add a personal touch to your quilt.

You may have a definite idea for a theme right at the beginning, or one can develop as you go along. You can start with some of the blocks that will fit in with any theme and maybe a simple border unit, then decide on the theme blocks later. Appliqué and foundation paper-pieced blocks are especially good at conveying a theme.

For example, a **north woods** theme could contain blocks with animals, trees, leaves, cabins, and wildflowers.

A **garden** theme could be flower-filled and contain paper-pieced flowers, appliquéd flowers, and baskets of flowers as well as watering cans, butterflies, ladybugs and birds...even frogs!

A **wildflower garden** theme might feature butterflies, hummingbirds, lady slippers, and rhododendrons, or other native plants that grow in your area.

A **nature lover** has lots to choose from—birds, animals, trees, flowers, and so on.

A **Japanese** theme could include kimonos, fans, and teapots.

Houses on a hillside and grapevines help carry out a **Tuscan** theme.

A **nautical** theme might include sea animals or ships.

Simply Dynamic Sampler Quilts ❀ Marianne L. Hatton

A **bird lover** could use pieced or appliquéd bird blocks and maybe a birdhouse, trees, or even a cat (safely in a window).

A **summertime** theme could be fun with ice-cream cones, umbrellas, watermelons, beach thongs, bathing suits, and plenty of sunshine.

Hearts convey a lovely sentiment to include in your theme and there can never be too many to show our love for the things we hold dear.

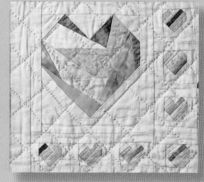

A **cat lover** could piece and appliqué many cats... and perhaps a mouse or two. Likewise, a **dog lover** could portray pooches.... and maybe a cat to chase.

Choose one of your favorites for a theme—flowers, season, pet, animal, holiday, activity, house, garden, food, color—or any combination of favorites. Or go with no particular theme at all, just a compilation of some of the things you love and that are meaningful to you. That gives you lots to choose from, anything from roosters to roses. The choices are endless!

Choosing Fabrics

I know it sounds rather daunting to be asked right off the bat to come up with at least 20 fabrics to begin your quilt! Using many fabrics ensures the quilt will take on a much more interesting personality. The interest and appeal lie in the subtle complexity of many fabrics blending gently together. There are no barriers (sashing) to confine the blocks, so they meld into a cohesive whole.

I usually find that once the project gets underway, the advantages of having an even greater variety of fabrics is clear. My students invariably collect many more fabrics, often having between 30 and 40 when all is said and done!

Even before we talk about picking a color scheme, let's discuss those elements that are important to know when hunting for your fabrics for this or any project. Although many of us prefer to choose fabric on an intuitive basis, I am going to suggest a little different approach.

Understanding Value

Whether you choose to work within a monochromatic color scheme or choose a combination of colors, understanding the concept of value is all important and plays a big role in the outcome of these and most other quilts you will make in the future.

So then, what exactly is value? Value, simply defined, **is the degree of lightness or darkness.** The very best way to look at and understand value in fabric terms is to assess the fabrics in relation to one another.

> **Tip** It is important to select fabrics in a wide range of values from light to dark. Those that are **very** dark or **very** light, that might be called the "extreme" fabrics, are often more difficult to find but make a real difference in the quilt. They help provide the depth that makes the individual elements stand out.

You will need the most fabrics in the very-light range. They make for an extremely interesting background and offer many choices as you piece the different elements. The light fabrics used in the background and at the edges of your blocks will enable the design elements to "float."

An exercise you can do with your own fabrics to really get a good understanding of value is one we do in my classes. We take a big group of fabrics—about 40 or more if possible, not necessarily in the same color family—and pile them in the center of a table. Then we arrange them in order, from lightest to darkest. It is a worthwhile exercise and always produces some surprises and uncertainties as to where a particular piece of fabric belongs in the lineup.

There are always fabrics that are more difficult to assess. The way to find their place is to lay them **across** the group, then try to gauge their place. Sometimes a "fuzzy look" helps—squinting or taking off your glasses to establish the placement.

There are some fabrics that fool the eye with very stark contrasts of light and dark. Such fabrics don't seem to play well with others. Although you want the range from light to dark, you really need the changes to happen from fabric to fabric, and not within one piece of fabric.

Another easy exercise is to work with a group of fabrics all in a similar color. Choose three to five fabrics and arrange them in order from the darkest to the lightest, folding them so strips of equal size are visible. Now choose three to five more and see where they fit in. Add in five more, and five more. Excellent! You might end up with an array looking something like this.

This set did indeed become the palette for a quilt (can you tell which one?) although many changes occurred along the way.

Start with 5 fabrics.

Add more...

Add some more...

And even more.

*T*ip If you are unsure of how well your fabrics are working and you have access to a copy machine, line up some of your fabrics with equal amounts showing and make a black-and-white copy of them. Or take a digital photograph of your fabrics, put it into a photo program, and use the Black/White option to see the values.

Playing with all these fabrics is a useful task. By the end of the exercises you'll be ready to tackle the fabric shops.

Choosing a Color Scheme

Sometimes you just need a particular fabric to speak to you as the starting point for a collection of fabrics with which to work. Picking colors you simply love and want to work with can begin a successful palette. Sometimes a fabric that is perfect for the border becomes the impetus for the rest of the quilt. This happened when I decided to use the leafy green palm frond fabric for COOL AND SHADY (page 32).

Doak pattern credits page 94

RASPBERRY SORBET, 47" x 47". *Made by Barbara Clifton, Sudbury, MA.*

Doak, Fons & Porter, and Rolfe pattern credits page 94

SHADES OF LAVENDER, 37" x 49". *Made by Ann B. Moses, Wayland, MA.*

Browsing in a fabric store without feeling pressure to buy can suddenly produce a winner. A favorite color can provide inspiration as in SHADES OF LAVENDER. Seeing another quilt that inspires you can set off a hunt for similar colors. One beautiful thing in your life can trigger an idea. A lovely picture of a collection of blue and white china inspired me to choose the fabrics for OF PEACE AND PORCELAIN (page 30).

Sally Cameron's ITALIAN MOSAIC (page 19) was inspired by just two fabrics. We went "shopping" in her own fabric collection and found 45 more! We drew in the colors in the first two fabrics and the result was magic.

OPPOSITE: ITALIAN MOSAIC, 68½" x 92". *Designed and made by Sally Cameron, Plymouth, MN.*

Old calendars, a special birthday card, art books, even magazine advertisements may suggest a color scheme. Develop a scheme from one of your own pictures. A photograph taken in autumn of the vineyards in Victoria, Australia, was the inspiration for the group of fabrics for ...AND A KOOKABURRA IN A GUM TREE.

Rolfe and Hiney pattern credits page 94

...AND A KOOKABURRA IN A GUM TREE, *54" x 66". Made by the author.*

I keep fabrics grouped together and keep adding until the day I feel ready to begin work on a new piece. I started looking for fabrics for MY GARDEN when I found a tiny scrap of fabric in a particular green and lavender. I added a photo of flowers and one taken in South Africa of a purple garden wall. Then I found an old poem, beloved by my mother and hers before her, that gave me the name and the theme.

Davis & Shiffer and Doak pattern credits page 94

MY GARDEN, *45" x 53". Made by the author.*

One-Way Color Schemes

When the first classes made these sampler quilts, we used a one-way or monochromatic color scheme. I still like that idea—just pick one color! If you have 30 or more fabrics to select from, then the interest within the individual blocks will be derived from the use of many fabrics in a full value range of the same color (hue).

Take a closer look at these quilts and you will start to see the subtle variations. For example, in the Log Cabin blocks, you will see that each log is a different fabric. Many of the appliquéd designs have been set on a background composed of several different fabrics. In the Star blocks, each star point is a different fabric. This is subtle, as the shades of the fabrics chosen are similar, but it definitely adds to the overall interest of the quilt.

Two-Way Color Schemes

Another way to choose fabrics is to seek a second color influence on a color you would like to work with. I once gathered and brought to class all the green fabrics I owned, about 40 to 50 in all (which was altogether very odd as I am not at all partial to green and had never before made a quilt that could be called green). We sorted them into three distinctly separate piles of blue-greens, yellow-greens, and green-greens! If we chose to work with the blue-greens, the second color would be blue, and the fabric choices would expand to include those with both blue and green in them. The pool of fabric choices just got larger and more interesting.

What also works very well with these next generation sampler quilts is a subtle and harmonious grouping—called "analogous" in color theory books—defined as colors adjacent to one another on the color wheel; for example, blue and green, yellow and orange, purple and violet. These will almost always look pleasing together.

Multicolored Schemes

Three colors can also be the basis for your color scheme as long as you have them in darks, lights, and everything in between, with plenty of "bridge" fabrics (see the next section). When too many colors are used, the quilt may lack unity. Your goals are harmony and balance. Values and bridge fabrics will help you achieve that.

It is easier, somehow, to put together 30 fabrics for a quilt than it is to choose just three! How is this possible? When choosing only three fabrics, each must shoulder a greater share of the responsibility for the success of the quilt, whereas when there are 30, they can all relax a little as the load is shared. As you start to add more fabrics to the mix they begin to relate to one or two others in the group, though maybe not all at the same time. It becomes easier to find more fabrics that work into the color scheme.

Bridging the Gap —Speaking More Than One Color Language

When many multicolored fabrics are put together, there are many opportunities for fabrics to relate, or chat, with each other. That's why

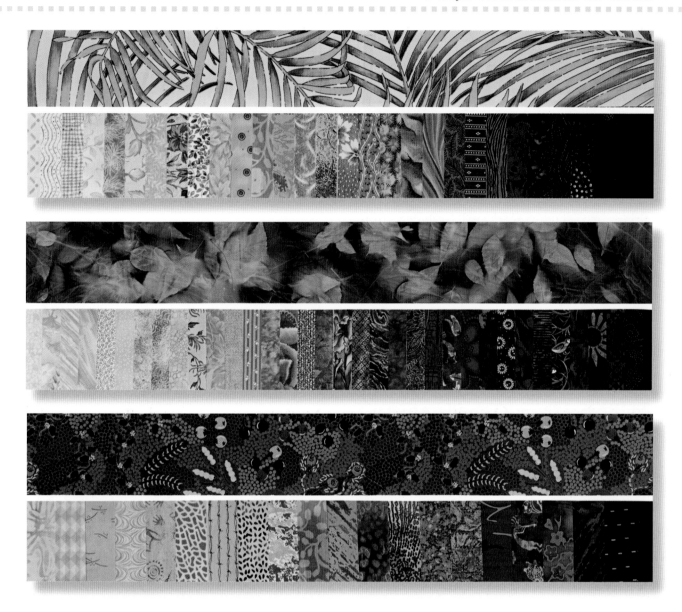

scrap quilts work so well. A bit of red in one fabric relates to a bit of red in another, those little spots of yellow resonate with the yellow leaves on a nearby section of the quilt, and so on.

The way I pick fabrics is to think in terms of their speaking different languages. Imagine the fabrics as a group of people at an international conference. If each conferee speaks only his or her own language, then they will have little to say to one another. If they speak another language as well, they are bound to find someone to chat with.

The same goes for fabric. If several of the fabrics speak more than their major color language, then they can act as translators for those that only speak a single color language. Some will manage only a smattering of another color language, but that will be all they need to get a conversation going! I call the fabrics with this interplay of colors **bridge fabrics** and seek them out whenever possible.

 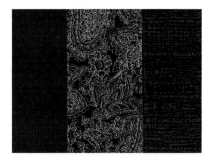 

The center "bridge" fabrics in the groups above get along well with both fabrics flanking them.

For a color scheme with several colors, as long as most of the fabrics have at least two of those colors in them (and have varied values), there will be a whole lot of mixing and blending going on, producing a lovely and lively quilt.

Additional Design Considerations

Visual Texture

It is also important to choose fabrics with differing visual texture. That really means they should vary somewhat in scale of print and color saturation. There is a lot to digest if you are new to this but, as you work more with fabric, it will become second nature to see them this way.

Scale is really easy to understand—large over-all pattern versus small. As you will be cutting the fabric into smaller pieces, any large-scale designs will tend to be lost, so in general, keep to small and medium prints for the body of the quilt. You could use a wonderful larger-scale print for the border.

Color saturation is the intensity of the pure dye of a color. Saturated fabrics can work well, but sometimes may be too overpowering next to more subtle fabrics. The fabulous array of batik fabrics can sometimes work well, but use them judiciously so as not to overwhelm their neighbors.

Shopping for Fabrics

Create a **color card** to take with you when shopping. Take a small swatch of each of the fabrics you have so far and stick them to a card arranged in value order from lightest to darkest. The goal should be to assemble about 20 to 30 fabrics in the range, starting with as little as ¼ yard of each.

Color card

You will be unlikely to find all you need in your own fabric collection or in just one store. Check out the quilt shops in your area. Each store has its own character, and it is remarkable how different the fabrics can be from store to store.

Choosing Block Sizes

I have chosen to base all the quilts in this book on blocks that are multiples of 4". It is necessary from the start of your sampler quilt to choose sizes for the blocks that will be compatible for ease of piecing them together into a whole. It's as simple as making sure that all the block sizes are multiples of the smallest block you decide to use.

For example, if the smallest blocks in the quilts are the 4" paper-pieced blocks, and your other blocks are all sized in a multiple of four (8", 12", 16" and so on), in theory everything should fit together like a jigsaw puzzle.

Divisions of that base size work as well. The checkerboard borders are made with 2" squares and are easy to adjust to fit the overall quilt size. Even a 6" block can be made to work into the grand scheme of things. The Kaleidoscope block is made up of 6" components. When four are pieced together the result is one 12" block. It works because 12 is divisible by 4.

Design Walls

I want to suggest early on the wonderful benefit of having a design wall. I quilted for years before I saw the advantages of having one. Once I realized how simple and inexpensive it was to make one, and what

a difference it made to my work, I wished I had done it years before.

A design wall allows you to view your work vertically. It works like the flannel boards you may have used in grade school. Whether an actual wall or not, a design "wall" allows you to arrange your patches or blocks, and step away (for a minute or a week or a month!) and mull over the design and color. Wherever you sew, there are several possibilities that may work if dedicating a wall is not an option for you.

The two most important considerations are to have a neutral color of a surface to which your fabric will cling. White or a light gray/beige both work. Flannel, felt, and cotton batting all answer the clingy surface requirement. Even the back of a vinyl tablecloth will work.

One simple way to make your own design wall is to buy two yards of 72" wide white felt (which is readily available and is quite inexpensive), sew a

hem along the top edge, and hang it on a curtain rod or dowel. Alternatively, put some grommets across the top and some hooks in the wall near the ceiling. Either way, it can be removed and stored or taken with you to class. I used a system like that for years when I sewed in a small corner of our family room and occupied just a little space for my craft.

Now that my family has grown up, I have expanded my sewing space and upgraded my design wall. I used a large piece of rigid foam insulation (available from DIY stores), nailed to the wall, and covered with both flannel and felt (to mask the pink color of the foam). The foam is available ¾"–1" thick in sheets 2' x 8'. It can easily be cut to fit the space you have available. Periodically, a once-over with a sticky lint roller will clear off loose threads and scraps.

If dedicating a wall is not an option for you, a piece of rigid foam insulation, or even foam-core, covered in felt or flannel, can be stored in the basement or a closet when it must be out of sight.

Doak, Fons & Porter, and Rolfe pattern credits page 94

TEAL SAMPLER, 51" x 64". *Made by Nancy Ross, North Eastham, MA.*

Resources and Pattern Sources

There are many places to seek designs and ideas. As this may be a project that develops over time and not the quilt that you need next month, I hope you will enjoy the treasure hunt of looking for theme block ideas. Try your local library, guild library, quilt shops, the Internet, or any of the many quilting magazines for patterns and inspiration.

Create Your Own Designs

I never ever thought of myself as having any artistic ability thanks to a careless first grade teacher who squelched any ambition I might have had otherwise! Happily, I discovered I could generate some designs if I put aside that thought and doodled until I had something I could work with. The flowers on MY GARDEN (page 21) are a case in point. You can certainly paper cut a snowflake or look to nature for appliqué designs. It is fulfilling to make your own patterns and it really makes your quilt your own.

A Final Word

If your quilt causes a viewer to wonder a little at its elements because it is not immediately obvious as a sampler, you have caught their attention. When its blocks are not all uniformly sized and the distinction between the blocks seems to disappear, they might try to puzzle over it longer. Perhaps they will see both its complexity and simplicity, taking in the multiple fabrics used, or wonder what made for such a striking quilt, given the simplicity of the color choice.

The more successful a quilt is, the longer a viewer will stand and look at it.

The GridMap:
The Guide, the Layout, the Grand Plan

Here is the essential key to putting the pieces of the quilt together—making a GridMap.

The two biggest differences between these next generation sampler quilts and traditional sampler quilts are the differing block sizes and the way in which they flow into one another rather than having some sort of visual separation such as sashing. (I'd like to say they flow "seamlessly"......but visually, definitely!)

Achieving a balanced look is the challenge, but you will shortly be underway to doing so with ease. You'll be making your blocks in sizes compatible with the grand plan—all finished block measurements in multiples or divisions of the same measurement (in our case, 4"). You will learn how to put a simple grid to work for you and will soon be able to create your own unique interpretation of this style of quilt. Please enjoy this step and don't skip it! When did you last get to play with paper, glue, and scissors?

Supplies

- Graph paper—4 squares per inch*
- Lead pencils—soft and hard, and sharpened
- Ruler
- Ultra-fine permanent marker
- Eraser
- Paper scissors
- Colored pencils (if you like, but plain lead pencils are best)
- Scotch® Repositionable Glue Stick 3M

*Not all squared graph paper is created equal. It's not essential to have precisely accurate paper for creating the GridMap but it is if you are also using the paper to create templates. Seek out a brand that has exact quarter-inch squares. Take along your grid ruler and line it up to see if the squares match it. Art and blueprint supply stores are sources for a better grade of graph paper.

Making the Pieces Fit

With that simple list, you now have the tools to make a scaled-down paper version of your quilt. Working to scale on a small piece of paper is the way to make sense of your layout design. Putting together a set of odd-sized blocks is a challenge for even the most experienced quilters, so hopefully this method will give you an "aha" moment! It is so much easier when you make mistakes on paper than on fabric. It is also easier to move around little bits of paper to position the quilt blocks than it is to move the actual fabric blocks.

Each component of the quilt—that is each block or unit you make—will be made on graph paper. The scale you will work with is very easy: one square of the graph paper equals one inch of your quilt.

Begin with a large sheet of graph paper, 11" x 14" if you have it, or tape two 8½" x 11" pieces together on the long side. Count the squares along the long and short sides. (My GridMap was 42 by 66 squares. Notice that both numbers are divisible by 2.) Each square represents one inch, so this provides a starting point for visualizing the size of your quilt. It may not fill up all the space or it might grow bigger.

Draw each of the planned blocks and components on a separate piece of graph paper as you go. Starting with the Log Cabin blocks is a good choice. Shade them in to indicate the dark areas and leave the light areas blank. This will convey their visual weight in the design and help you as you move around the pieces on the grid to determine your final arrangement. Keep the paper blocks safe and organized in a plastic envelope or zipper bag until you have enough to start playing with the layout.

I prefer using an ultra-fine permanent marker to outline the blocks and draw the seam lines, then use lead pencil to shade the blocks. You can use color pencils, but be careful not to let color get in the way of value. It is really only the light versus dark contrast that matters here.

You may also enjoy doing this part using a drawing program on the computer. I would suggest not putting all your energy into learning a

new program from scratch if it isn't already something you know how to use. You could also just draw the outlines and major construction lines of the blocks on the computer, and fill in the shading in pencil after you print them.

In order to start playing around with the placement, it isn't necessary that you have all the blocks made, but it makes sense to have the major pieces done. By the time you finish piecing your blocks, you will have all of them rendered on paper, drawn to scale. They will resemble your blocks in design and value, and will represent all the pieces you have made in fabric.

Cut around the individual blocks and units—finished size, with no outside seam allowance. Using the wondrous restickable gluestick, start placing the paper pieces on the base grid sheet, secure in the knowledge that you can move them around on the base grid to your heart's content, because they will just peel up and re-stick so easily.

One of the objectives is to see what spaces you may have to fill once all the major pieces are placed. Usually they are small pieces and easy and fun to make (page 87)—little strips of triangles or small foundation paper-pieced squares that can add to the theme you have chosen. Keep playing and you'll start to get a feel for the eventual size of your quilt, but don't get hung up here. It will become clearer as your quilt evolves.

Planning the Layout

A second objective of using your GridMap is to create a balanced, harmonious layout for the blocks. The things to consider as you look at your pieces are twofold: first, you will be looking to balance the placement of the pieces around the quilt; second, assess them in terms of their "visual weight." This weight will largely depend on the value within the block—how much there is of the darker shades versus the lighter ones. These may be new ideas for you in the making of quilts, but they are easy and logical things to visualize and to decide.

Repetition

There's strength in numbers, so use repeat motifs, for example, a checkerboard grid or other pattern for the top and bottom inner borders. Repeating an idea in differing techniques has a strong effect. For example, use foundation paper-pieced flowers and appliquéd flowers in the same quilt.

Small blocks, like 4" paper-pieced blocks, repeat particularly well; groups of three work better than two. Small elements gain strength by being repeated. The larger elements work better as singles.

Unity

Unity will be achieved through your fabric and color choices and by distributing your variety of fabrics throughout the quilt. Your theme blocks will contribute to unity as well.

Balance

Balance will be achieved by looking at the elements of your quilt for pieces that have similar design features or similar visual weight. You may need to add a block (that doesn't necessarily have to fit with your theme) or even remove and replace a piece that is not working. My students have gotten used to "voting something off the island" for the greater impact the quilt will have without it!

In OF PEACE AND PORCELAIN, the upper-left appliqué and the lower-right Log Cabin seem to carry a similar visual weight, but the Log Cabin is definitely heavier and belongs on the lower part

Doak pattern credits page 94

OF PEACE AND PORCELAIN, 54" x 67½".
Made by the author.

of the quilt. They balance each other out. I decided to make the three linear 8" blocks in the lower left-hand corner to counterbalance the three 8" circle blocks in the upper right. Note I didn't feel I needed more curves, but chose the same size blocks that also had the "heavy" looking corners. I wish now I had positioned the center circle block slightly differently so as to create the same zigzag effect that is going on in the blocks on the lower left; or those blocks could have been rotated to resemble the circle orientation.

cal border. The kaleidoscope is light and airy. The Log Cabin appears heavier, so it settles lower down on the quilt. The other pieces have resolved into a lovely, gentle balance.

The important thing to remember is that you are looking for balance rather than symmetry—the way in which the elements relate to each other in terms of their respective size and visual weight. This kind of play to rearrange the blocks can go on until you are satisfied with the arrange-

Another choice was to have the six small trees balance the one large pine tree as both designs have sharp, pointed elements. The two small lines of triangle filler strips on the outer edges balance each other. Note also the two large offset stars on the body of the quilt. I like that they are not lined up directly with one another, and that they reappear, smaller now, in the four corners. And so it goes. There is always more than one way to do these things, of course, but eventually you will settle for what seems to look best.

Look at the delicate balance achieved in Japanese Impressions (right). The checkerboards are a more subtle insert throughout the quilt, and in the two corners the "moons" serve instead as something of an asymmetri-

JAPANESE IMPRESSIONS, 45" x 59". Made by Cynthia Ross Lauer, Sudbury, MA.

Hiney pattern credits page 94

Doak pattern credits page 94

COOL AND SHADY, 39½" x 47". *Made by the author.*

ment. It is so beneficial to play with the design before stitching the blocks together. It will save time, frustration, and fabric to plan the quilt this way as you go along. It doesn't guarantee that you won't be using your seam ripper somewhere along the line, but there will be fewer ripping episodes!

You can arrange one design, photocopy the layout, and then take it apart and rearrange the blocks. Once you have several options copied you will have a good basis for comparison. Did I mention yet that two of my favorite tools are a copy machine and a digital camera? These two "toys" allow you to play with different design options.

Here are four different options for the small quilt COOL AND SHADY, along with the final choice.

When I was making this quilt, I was away from home, without my usual tools and resources. It was so much smaller than the first such quilt I had made, I just sewed it together without making a grid, figuring I couldn't go far wrong because surely I knew what I was doing! Well, it looked awful. I took it apart completely, took my own advice, made the grid, and ended up with a much better, balanced quilt!

The final decision on your arrangement will be made once you have all your blocks made and you can lay them out on a design wall. Then the colors will come into the decision-making. If you are working on a larger-sized quilt, the balancing act is sometimes easier as you have more options to work with than in the smaller version, so there may be a reward for taking on a bigger quilt.

The important thing is to get started, both sewing and working on the grid.

Please don't skip making your Grid-Map. I have seen so many of the quilts undergo radical changes—from choppy to resolved—when the paperwork was done first, followed by tweaking on the design wall!

I tested the GridMap in class, then on my sister-in-law (more sister, less in-law), who is one of my toughest critics. She was ready to put her blocks together for MEMORIES FROM DOWN UNDER, but I asked her to try the GridMap first. She agreed with great reluctance and grumbled about it as she worked, but gradually the mutterings turned to appreciative little hmmphs, and eventually to outright approval, enjoyment, and finally wholesale endorsement of the process.

I've provided some pre-drawn blocks on page 34 for you to use in addition to the ones you draw yourself.

We will be taking another look at the GridMap later on after you have the pieces ready to arrange. Happy sewing!

Causee, Doak, and Rolfe pattern credits page 94

MEMORIES FROM DOWN UNDER, *41" x 55". Made by Shirley Lawrence Jones, Witbank, South Africa.*

Simply Dynamic Sampler Quilts ♣ Marianne L. Hatton

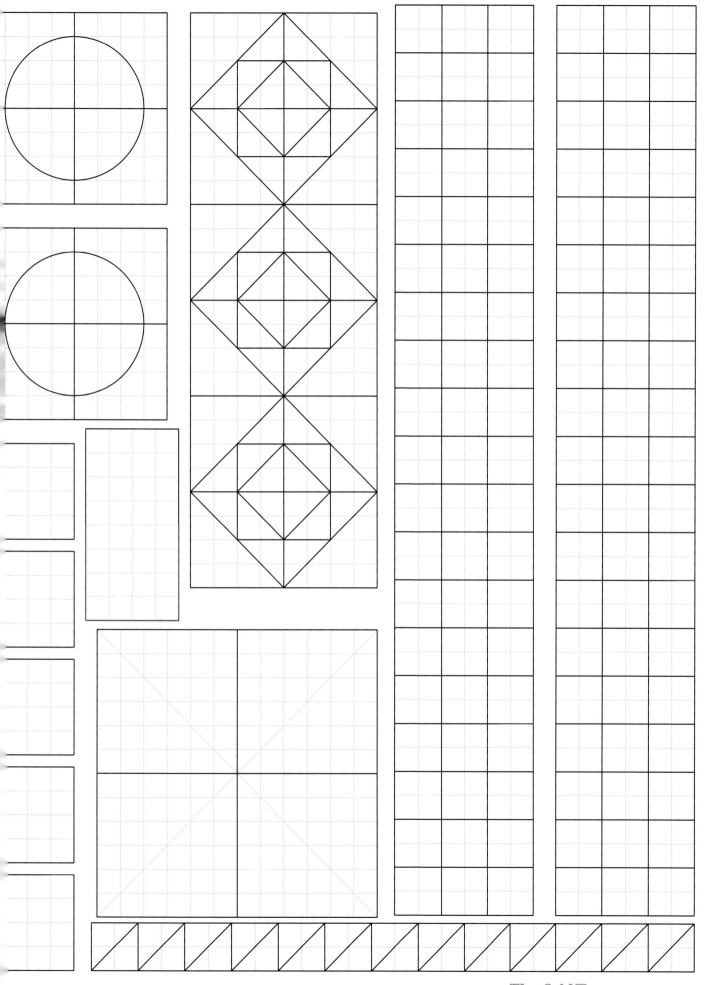

Templates and Drafting

It's time to get rid of the fear factor!

As I go about the business of teaching, I find that quilters can be broadly categorized into two groups—the ARCs and the BRCs. What am I talking about? Well, there are those who started quiltmaking **after** the arrival of the truly amazing rotary cutter—the ARCs—and those quilters who came **before** the rotary cutter was a staple item in every quiltmaker's workbox—the BRCs!

The rotary cutter is absolutely one of the pivotal breakthrough inventions of the quilting world. I doubt any of us can imagine being without one!

Before there were rotary cutters, one needed to draw upon a little simple geometry to make the patterns and then the templates for each different piece of the block we were making. After the advent of rotary cutters, this skill got somewhat mothballed. That meant patterns and sizes for quilt blocks were presented using predetermined measurements with seam allowances included. The choice of block size was made for us.

All of this is a very good thing, but two things have happened. The first is that many quilters do not know how to alter the block sizes determined by pattern designers. The second downside is that many quilters are unnecessarily fearful of trying to use templates. If you're a BRC, templates were a given, but an understanding of templates is **still** an important skill for ARCs to have.

Knowing how to use templates allows you the freedom to depart from preset sizes of blocks, giving you complete control over the size of whatever you are making. You will find *templates are not nearly as difficult* as you may think! Some of the quilting world's most respected and influential teachers have told me that they often find students in their workshops employing the most cumbersome techniques to avoid the "dreaded template" when, in fact, the use of a template could actually make their task much simpler!

I am most certainly not suggesting that you give up using rotary-cutting techniques. But I hope you will try using templates, even just this once, on the curved-seam blocks, the Kaleidoscope, and maybe for any straight-seam blocks you add in. Because you will be using so many different fabrics in your sampler quilt, it is easier to mark and cut out individual pieces with templates.

If template talk is new territory for you, in a nutshell, **a template is simply an outline of an individual patch required for the quilt block you are making, which may or may not include the seam allowance.** I am a fan of stitching on a pre-marked stitching line for accurate results, and for this reason these templates will be made **without** the seam allowance added. An added plus is that they can be used for both hand and machine piecing.

Understanding templates goes hand in hand with understanding how to draft, or draw, a quilt block. If you are a BRC quilter and this is old hat to you, please feel free to skip this chapter, although you might like to stay tuned to refresh your memory on working with templates that do not have seam allowance added.

In the "old days" when I started quilting, we used to make templates from cardboard and graph paper. Now there are excellent sheets of gridded, semi-transparent plastic specifically designed for templates. EZ® Quilting Gridded Template Plastic is the type I prefer to use. It comes in 12" x 18" sheets and is ruled with super accurate fine lines with ⅛" and ¼" lines differentiated and the full inch lines very clearly defined. Avoid the rolls of graphed template plastic if you can, as they are very hard to get to lie flat.

One huge advantage to working with templates is that you can choose the size of your block, and make the templates accordingly. If you see a 9" block you would like in the quilt, which does not fit into a 4" multiple scheme, you can scale it down to a 6" block (and make two or four to fit the multiple plan) or up to a 12" block. It takes only the minimal amount of simple geometry to get started. Now, don't get nervous—it is elementary school stuff and you can certainly do it!

Supplies

- ¼" ruled graph paper (Very accurate paper with heavier lines for the inch marks is available at art supply stores.)
- 12" x 18" sheet gridded template plastic (available at most quilt shops)
- A sharp pencil
- An extra-fine permanent marking pen
- A ruler

I suggest drawing/drafting the block you are going to make on a sheet of graph paper first. Once you have it right, draw the parts you need on the template plastic. You won't always need to draw the whole block onto the plastic as a block may have many patches but only require a few templates, as the shapes are repeated.

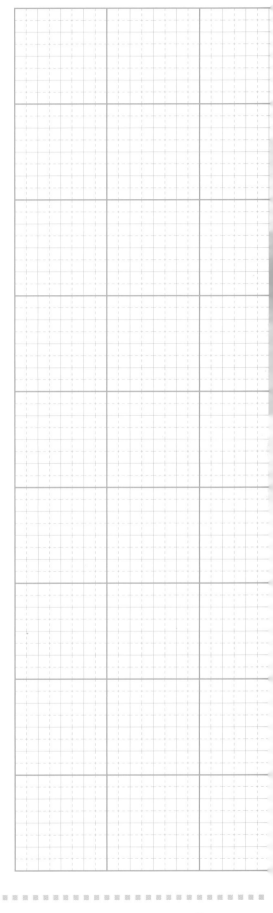

This is a Four-Patch block. Divided this way it becomes the Broken Dishes block. You'd need just one template. The template could be a 2" triangle, making it a 4" block; a 4" triangle, making it an 8" block; a 5" triangle making it a 10" block; and so on. By the size of your one template, you can make the block *any size you want!*

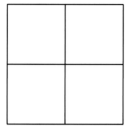 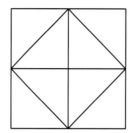 

This next block is slightly more complex, but also easy. Although there are 20 patches, there are actually only two different templates needed to make the block—a large triangle and small triangle.

 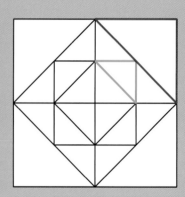

Suppose you want the block to be 8" x 8". The large triangle will have 4" "legs" (the two sides next to the right angle). The hypotenuse, the diagonal line opposite the right angle, is an odd measurement that **you will not have to worry about or calculate**. The small triangle legs are 2"—half the size of the large triangle legs.

If you want to make the block larger, perhaps 12", then you need to change the dimensions accordingly—to 6" and 3". If you want a 4" block, the dimensions would be 2" and 1".

Some blocks get a lot more complicated than this, but most can fit into one of several size grids, usually based on the number of squares across each edge. The grids are usually named the same way, although sometimes they are also referred to by the number of squares in the block.

You can go further and divide a four-patch into an eight-patch or a five-patch into a ten-patch. The block with 6 across the top is just a 3 x 3 or nine-patch grid simply divided further. You get the picture.

Identify a block by counting the number of squares across the top of the block to determine its grid. Use that grid to plot out the block, making the squares in the grid any size you want.

Now you can take the same set of grids and envision them with lines that break them up further into distinctive looking quilt blocks.

Once you start to think of each block in its grid format you will have at your fingertips the ability to draft any block into any size you need it to be, and make the pattern and templates to make it. What freedom!

All you need to remember is to draw the block the size you want, and then to make as many divisions as you need to draft the design you want.

Thus, a Six-Patch block could be made with 1½" divisions for a 9" finished block, with 2" divisions for a 12" block, with 2½" divisions for

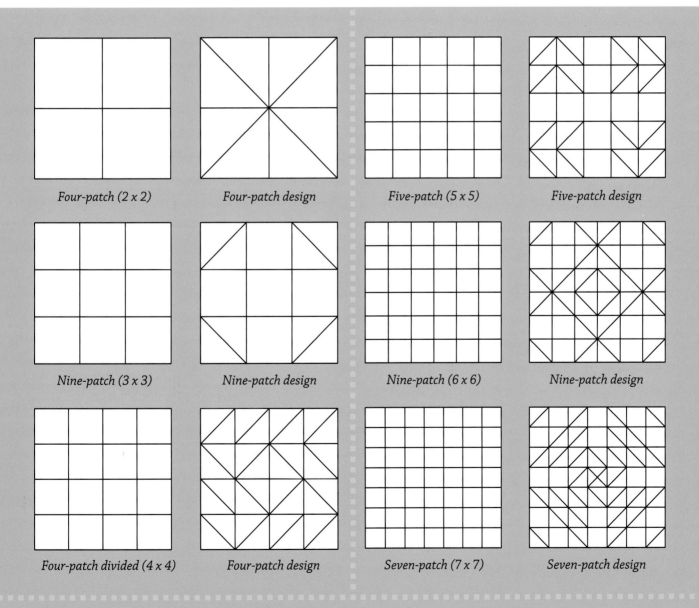

Four-patch (2 x 2)   *Four-patch design*   *Five-patch (5 x 5)*   *Five-patch design*

Nine-patch (3 x 3)   *Nine-patch design*   *Nine-patch (6 x 6)*   *Nine-patch design*

Four-patch divided (4 x 4)   *Four-patch design*   *Seven-patch (7 x 7)*   *Seven-patch design*

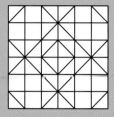

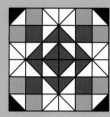

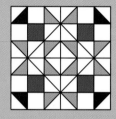

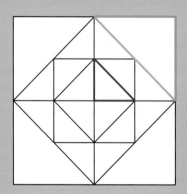

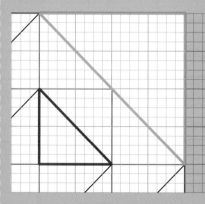

a 15" block, and so on. **It is so very important** to doodle with pencil and paper and to know that you are able to create something beyond the limits of a pattern in a set size.

Try this exercise when you start playing around with blocks. Take any quilt block you like drawn in line form. Duplicate it and then shade it two different ways, and you will have two distinctly different quilt blocks.

Also try playing with different fabric combinations, even with no intent to use them. Just experimenting will widen your sense of what may or may not work together and will surely produce some surprises.

How to Make Templates

The first thing to know about piecing a block accurately is that you have to start with accurate templates, so do all in your power to make sure that they are!

If you were going make this block and wanted it to be 8" x 8", first draw it out on a sheet of ¼" graph paper. Mark the two different triangles that make up the block.

Next, take a sheet of template plastic, and lay it over the drawing, lining up the markings on the plastic with those on the graph paper. You may find that the markings on the plastic sheet are more accurate than the graph paper itself, so it is actually better to go by that than by the graph paper. (If you are using a really good engineering-quality graph paper however, it should be perfect.) Trace the shapes you need, drawing them carefully with **a fine permanent marker**. If it is difficult to see the marker on the template plastic, make a mark at the points of the triangle to indicate the start/end points of the lines you need.

A note about curved seams: Any time you have a seam with a curve in it, you need to mark the templates where the seams should line up with registration marks. Do this along the curve *before* you cut the templates apart. (See page 69.)

Cut out the templates precisely on the drawn lines with scissors or a rotary cutter dedicated to paper and plastic. Simple.

If you use a rotary cutter, you'll need to draw the templates with a little space between them so you have enough room to cut a little beyond the end of each line. Position the ruler **over** the template, rather than on the outside of it, keep your hand firmly on the ruler, and **slice twice** to be sure you have gone all the way through the plastic.

Mark the templates with their size, the name of the block you are making, and arrows to indicate the grain line(s) to be aware of as you cut. Add your name or initials, especially if you are in a class, to keep track of them.

A word about grain line. Fabric has threads that go in two directions. The WARP runs lengthwise, parallel to the selvage. The WEFT runs crosswise. When placing templates for cutting, it is generally considered desirable to have as many sides of the template on the "straight of grain" as possible, that is, lined up with the warp or weft.

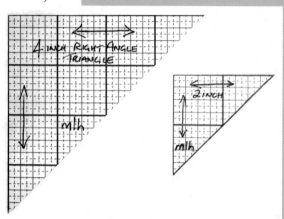

Quilters Newsletter and Rolfe pattern credits page 94

LEFT: A MARINER'S DREAMS, 53" x 65". Made by Katherine S. Cromwell, Wayland, MA.

Piecing Techniques

"Fast is fine, but accuracy is better."
Wyatt Earp

Different strokes for different folks and different piecing techniques for different applications. Hand piecing, machine piecing, seams marked and pieces rough-cut, seams incorporated but not marked on the piece, strip-piecing, paper piecing...lots of choices, and no one piecing technique works best for everything. All the techniques should lead to the same end result—**an accurate block the size it was intended to be.**

I think some piecing techniques are better suited to certain applications than others, and I will point those differences out as we go along. An interesting option would be to piece some of the quilt by hand and some by machine. We all develop our favorites, but it is good to be versatile and be able to do things differently when appropriate. It's up to you to decide which ways you prefer.

Piecing by Hand

It is probable that you will be planning on making your sampler quilt using a sewing machine. It may come as a surprise to you that in spite of being thoroughly competent in the handling of a sewing machine, many people opt to piece by hand! It need not be as slow a process as you envision. One of the best things about piecing by hand is that it is portable, and that you can while away otherwise idle time piecing wherever you want.

I made great strides on many of my quilts hand piecing while watching my sons' sports practices and long games, in waiting rooms, and traveling. I have family overseas and this means long distance travel is a given. My one dread is being stuck for hours in transit somewhere with nothing to do! It is also good to have something with you to do at your destination when your machine is at home. For this quilt, you might try piecing part by hand and part by machine for good measure.

Supplies for Hand Piecing

- Template plastic—with a grid (or plain plastic and very accurate ¼" graph paper)
- A Sharpie® fine point permanent marker
- A sharp, soft, pencil 4B
- A Pigma® 01 archival permanent marker
- A sheet of emery cloth—fine grade
- Pins
- Fabric
- Thread
- Something to cut your thread with—a little pair of scissors or, if traveling, perhaps a pendant thread cutter

It is best to have a line to follow when hand piecing, so start by making templates without seam allowances as described in the last chapter (page 40).

Practice on a simple block first—maybe just a Nine-Patch to start—with 2" x 2" templates and two contrasting fabrics.

Marking the Fabric

When you draw around templates onto the fabric, you will be marking the *stitching* line on the wrong side of the fabric. Place a piece of fine grade emery cloth (a cloth-backed version of sandpaper available at hardware stores) under the fabric. The rough surface of the emery cloth will keep the fabric from slipping or dragging as you mark it.

Place the template on the straight grain of the fabric. Make a tiny but definite dot at each corner for matching up later, or extend the lines a little, making an X, as shown. Marking these first will make your tracing more accurate, and not susceptible to being dragged out of place.

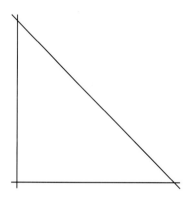

Use either a very sharp, soft pencil or Pigma pen, and trace around the template. What, you say, permanent? Yes. It may seem radical, but I like the consistently fine line it gives. I was taught to use it for accurately marking appliqué pieces by a fine teacher and decided to try it for templates. So far I haven't found a reason not to use it. Test the marker first, and use a light, quick touch as you mark so it does not have a chance to seep into the fabric.

If your template includes a curved seam, be sure to draw the registration marks as well (page 70).

For a Nine-Patch, mark four 2" x 2" squares on the lighter fabric and five darker squares (or the other way around). Draw the squares just over a half-inch away from each other to allow enough space for the seam allowance. You can trust your eye and "rough cut" them apart, or draw in a ¼" seam allowance and cut along the second drawn line.

Piecing a Nine-Patch by Hand

Lay the cut squares out so you know what goes next to what. Pin them to a sheet of paper if you like.

Pick up two adjacent pieces and place them right sides together. Take a pin, pierce the top fabric exactly at the dot at the one end of the seam you are going to sew, then through the corresponding dot on the lower fabric. Make sure the two fabrics are "pushed" together on the pin, then anchor it into the fabric so it holds. Repeat

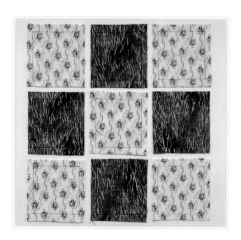

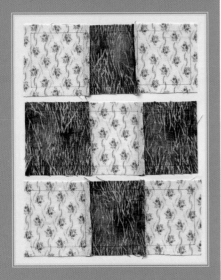

stitching line

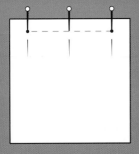

at the opposite end of the seam. Then pin again in the center of the seam using the lines as the guide this time, being just as careful to match them exactly.

When pinning curved seams together, first match them at the ends of the seam, then at the registration marks, and then possibly in between as well. Occasionally it is necessary to use a registration mark on a straight seam.

You will be stitching along the seam line you have marked, so you always know you are on track. Use a slim needle, one strand of thread, no knot, and small running stitches no larger than ⅛". Begin with three stitches sewing *toward the dot from within the seam.* Remove the pin and stitch through the dot, then turn and stitch to the dot at the other end of the seam, removing the pin and stitching through the dot. Finally, take three stitches back over the seam stitching. *You do not stitch into the seam allowance at all.*

In the same way, add the third piece to the row, then construct the next two rows. Check each seam for accuracy.

To join the rows, pin two rows together at the ends, through the dots, as before. Now take a pin through the dot at the first intersection you will reach when sewing, and holding the seam out of the way, find the dot on the lower piece, also holding its seam out of the way. Join the dots by pinning. Do the same with the dots at the next seam.

Place an additional pin on the lines in between the seams. Proceed with the stitching as before. When you get to the dot, take one small back stitch, then release the seam from the pin, pass the needle through the seam allowance at its base, find and match the dots with a pin at the start of the next section, then stitch up to the next seam. Repeat! Add the third row of patches.

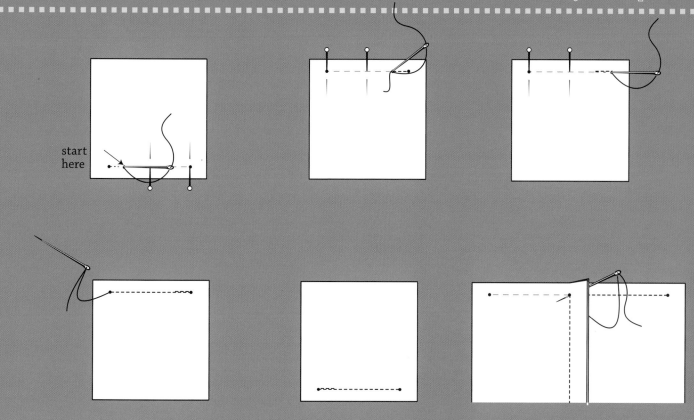

start
here

When sewing the rows together, I especially like keeping the seam allowances free so I can decide later where I want them to be pressed. Then I can always distribute the bulk of the seams evenly. It's especially good to be able to manipulate seam allowances this way on a more complicated block.

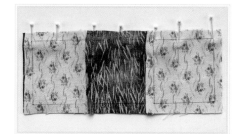

Pressing and Blocking

Piece First, Press Later! I choose not to press the block until I have pieced it, preferring to "block it," just as you might a piece of knitting. **I do the same for both hand and machine piecing when using templates without seam allowances.**

If it is intended to be a 6" block, then by golly, it will be, by the time it is blocked and pressed! I have a grid marked on my ironing board for this purpose. I place the block face down and pin through the marked lines on the outer edges of the block into the lines on the ironing board corresponding to the intended measurements. Then

I steam press the block, committing my seams wherever I want them. I leave it to cool a few minutes to "set." Then I press from the front for a nice finish.

This process allows for the natural give in the fabric to work and for you to avail yourself of the "ease" factor in the fabric, and beat it into submission...gently!

Generally seams are pressed to one side or the other, seldom open. Sometimes you have to flip-flop the pressing direction in the middle of the seam. At first I was distressed when this happened, but once I saw that on the front it is usually indiscernible, I was not concerned. Having a nice, flat intersection to work with is better.

"Pressing" is different from "ironing." Pressing means just that—the iron presses down. Ironing back and forth can distort the fabric, which is significant on small patches when you are aiming for accuracy.

Accurate Machine Piecing Using Templates without Seam Allowances

I first learned this technique from Marla Mc-Cormick-Snyder, who taught us we could even piece tiny, skinny points on Mariner's Compass blocks using templates without the seam allowance added in. I enjoy the flexibility and accuracy it provides. You use the seam line as the guide rather than the cut edge of the fabric. This is the method I recommend for the Kaleidoscope and curved-seam blocks as the outcome tends to be more consistently accurate.

Templates

Templates are made the same way as for hand piecing, cutting them *the exact finished size and shape of the patch being sewn.* You can draw/trace/copy the block with all its required pieces onto graph paper, trace the patches needed onto template plastic, and cut them out accurately. Mark grain lines when appropriate. Transfer the design to the fabric by drawing around the template, using a very sharp pencil or a Pigma pen. Make dots at the corners for pinning. Cut the pieces out, adding the ¼" seam allowance.

Pinning the Seams

Pick up the first two pieces to be stitched, place them right sides together, and using a fine, slim pin, pin through the dot at the end of the seam. Push the fabrics together up the shaft of the pin, then push the pin through to the top again, taking up only a small amount of fabric. Repeat at the end of the seam, and pin between the dots with as many pins as you need to keep the pieces firmly anchored. Do as good a job as possible of keeping the seams aligned.

Stitching

You'll stitch only on the drawn stitching lines and up to the intersections, not into the seam allowances. This will allow for absolute flexibility when it comes to choosing the direction you want the seams to be pressed. With the sewing machine, begin stitching from ¼" along the seam line *toward* the dots. Remove the pin and leave the needle down in the fabric at the dot. Pivot the work, stitch the length of the seam, pivot again, and stitch ¼" *back along* the seam. It may seem strange, but it works!

Block and press the same as with hand piecing (page 45).

Accurate Machine Piecing Using Templates with Seam Allowances

When you make templates with the seam allowance built in, you will be transferring the *cutting* line to the fabric. Draw around the template onto fabric with a consistently sharp pencil or a Pigma pen. Cut out the pieces exactly on the lines, as the cut edge will serve as your guide when piecing.

You need to establish a way to stitch a consistent ¼" seam. Unless you do, your blocks will be inconsistent and cause you unnecessary frustration! Use a ¼" machine foot or move the needle position to where the seam measurement is accurate. Another option is to place a piece of tape on the machine ¼" to the right of the needle to serve as a guide for the raw edge of the fabric. Try out the different options and find the one that works best for you. The success of any quilt is greatly enhanced by consistency and accuracy.

The biggest difference between this and the templates-without-seam-allowance technique is that you will stitch from end to end of the patches, pressing the seams as you go and not waiting until the entire block is pieced. Each seam should be pressed either using an iron, a small plastic pressing tool, or even your finger nail to establish that the crease is in the right place before moving on to the next seam.

A general rule is to press the seams toward the darker fabric, but it's more *important to reduce the bulk at the intersections of seams as much as you can.* I always used steam to press and was skeptical when my teaching friend Brigitte Lee in Singapore did not even have a steam iron in her shop! Forced to iron dry, I became quite a convert. Now I use a dry iron when I am piecing as it minimizes distortion. However, I usually steam when I'm "blocking" (page 45).

Piecing accurately is a skill that will develop as you progress. It is important to be as precise as is possible for the satisfaction you will derive from a job well done, and for the ease of piecing together you will achieve. Overlook small inaccuracies, as obsession is not healthy either. If when you stand back from a piece it is not a glaring mistake, I don't think it should be pulled out. One of my students always reminds me, if it can't be seen from a trotting horse, then it's OK! Sometimes that is a stretch for me—a stickler for accuracy—but it is also good to know when to let it go!

Lovely, Linear,
Log Cabin Blocks

Japanese Impressions, detail

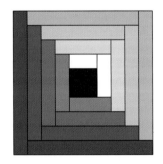

Standard Log Cabin block

The Log Cabin block is a good place to begin. It will use most, if not all, of your fabrics right away and help you become more familiar with the subtle values of your fabrics as you see how they relate and behave next to one another. That in turn will help you make choices as to which will be the best fabrics for other elements as your quilt progresses.

The traditional Log Cabin block begins with a center square, then same-width strips of fabric are added—light strips on two adjacent sides and dark strips on the opposite two sides. Strips are added in a continuous "spiral" around the center until the desired size is reached. You will notice, however, that all of the quilts use a slightly different Log Cabin block, where the logs are different widths on the light and dark sides.

The best thing about this amazing block is the effect of a shadow that the use of light and dark fabrics creates in different arrangements.

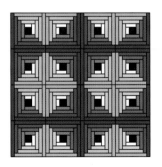 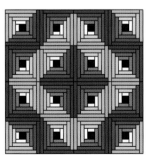 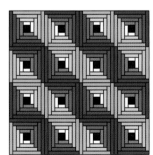 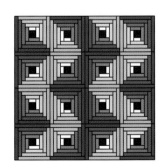

Different block arrangements

Simply Dynamic Sampler Quilts ♣ Marianne L. Hatton

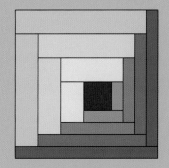

Off-center Log Cabin block

The fascinating thing is that although there are only straight lines and sharp corners, the illusion of a curve is created as a result.

I first saw this off-center treatment in a quilt made by Maria McCormick-Snyder back in the late 1970s, and loved it. I suggest using this type of Log Cabin block for your sampler. You'll make four 6½" blocks and join them for a 12½" block (including seam allowance).

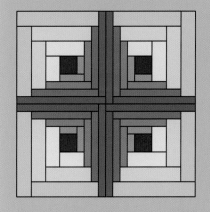

Cutting the Fabrics

If you are not already familiar with the rotary cutter, mat, and ruler, you will have become very good friends once you have cut all the strips for your Log Cabin blocks! Cut just one strip from each fabric to start. With about 20 to 30 fabrics, you will be able to do all or most of the four Log Cabin blocks with what you have. As you cut the strips, use the grid marking on the ruler as well as on the mat, to keep the strips straight. These strips incorporate the ¼" seam allowance. You are not using templates here.

For the center, cut a 1¾" strip from a medium or a dark fabric, then cut four squares 1¾" x 1¾".

Cut a 1" wide strip from each of your **dark, medium-dark, and medium fabrics**, cutting parallel to the selvage. You may need to cut more later if you run out, but this is a good set of strips to begin with.

Cut a 1½" wide strip from each of your **light and medium-light fabrics**.

Depending on your preferred way of working, lay out your strips in order near your machine, or use a drying rack to keep them neat as you work, or just plunk them in piles of lights and darks and select randomly as you go.

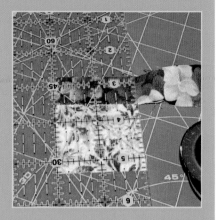

Piecing the Log Cabin block

Sewing the Blocks

Begin by stitching a narrow dark strip to one side of the center square. **Leave the strip the length it was when you cut it.** Use a dry iron to press the strip away from the square. Align your rotary ruler with the side of the square and trim off the excess strip.

Please note: Sometimes it is necessary to use all the options you have for keeping things in line—the edge of the starting fabric, the seam lines, and the edge of the new piece of fabric you have added, to get an accurate cut. If the cut is not square, then each successive fabric you add will be progressively more off kilter!

As you add strips, always go around in the same direction. Imagine the central square with a compass on it. If you just added a dark strip to the **east** side of the block, you'll add a different dark strip to the **south** side of the center square. Remember to keep the growing block from distorting as you press and trim.

Now it's time to use the lighter set of fabrics. Stitch a light strip to the **west** side, press and trim, then add a different light strip to the **north** side. Essentially, you are adding the strips in a clockwise rotation. And you will be noticing by now, how every other strip increases in length.

Continue adding the strips paying careful attention to placement of light and dark, until you have three light strips on two sides and four dark strips on the other two sides. Remember to make each strip from a different fabric for maximum variety.

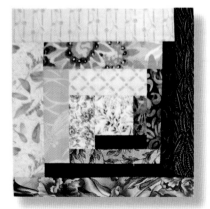

My Garden, *detail*

Use a medium strip among the darker fabrics to break up the really dark side a little. It is fine to repeat a fabric so that one fabric shows up more than once in the four blocks.

The block should measure 6½" x 6½" including seam allowances. If it is a little larger, don't worry, as it is easier to trim down without a problem. If it is smaller it may be a good time to assess just how accurate a quarter-inch seam your machine is giving you. It may be taking a fraction more than you think, and that fraction compounded will affect the whole finished block and later the quilt. When you join the four blocks, the goal is a perfect 12½" x 12½".

So, the first one is done and looks very nice, right? Now, make three more in the same way, varying the fabrics and working always on improving your accuracy. As you get to the outer strips, pay attention to which fabrics you add so as not to have the same fabrics in the last rows, ensuring a good mix. Sometimes I lay out the strips ahead of time to keep an eye on that.

Sometimes it is necessary to use all the options you have for keeping things in line

About Chain Piecing

This block is a great place to try chain piecing to make all four (or just the next three) Log Cabin blocks at the same time. To chain piece, you add the equivalent piece to each block in succession *without removing the fabrics from the machine.* Cut the strips you're adding a little longer than the piece you are adding to. This takes being ordered and careful, and remembering to use a different fabric each time. When you have added a strip to all four blocks, snip them apart, and press and trim. Then add the next strip to all four pieces, and so on and so on.

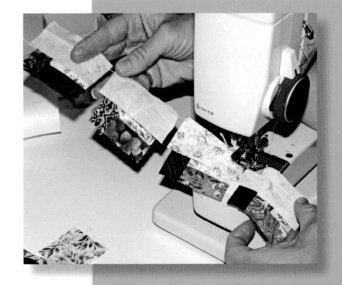

Blocking the Log Cabins

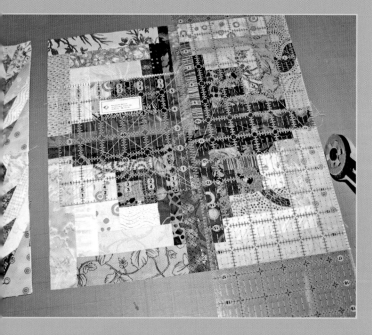

Trimming the Log Cabins

Joining the Blocks

Arrange the four blocks with the dark sides in the center, showing the soft curves where the darks and lights intersect. Join the blocks in two sets of two, pressing the seams in opposite directions, then join the two sets along a central seam so that the seam allowances butt up to one another. Press the central seam in one direction, or if it seems more appropriate, press the seam open.

Press first from the wrong side, then from the right side, remembering to press and not to iron. Pin the block to your gridded ironing surface to block. Use some steam now for a good crisp look.

Trim the entire block with the rotary cutter and ruler to be **exactly** 12½" square. A good way to do this is to measure 6¼" in each direction from the center seams, using your ruler to be sure it is square.

And there it is—your first full block. Put it onto the design wall, along with your inspirations, so you can admire it. Be proud and move on to the next assignment!

Simple Strip Piecing

Starting off and ending the body of the quilt with two inset strip-pieced borders is a fun and quick way to get a substantial chunk of the quilt done right away. Having them ready as you assemble all the varying parts of the quilt is useful. Visually, it is helpful to have them on the design wall as you look at, add, and arrange the different sections. You will already have the framework of the quilt in place, making for a cohesive look right from the start.

Most of the quilts in this book feature the checkerboard or a variation thereof. As with the Log Cabin block, this method of construction is rotary cut and incorporates the seam allowances.

Almost all the borders use a light/dark contrast plan. How long you make the borders will be your choice. On a smaller quilt, you could start with borders that are 28"–30" long, while on a larger version, about 40"–42". Because they are made with 2" units, it will be very easy to increase or decrease their size if you decide to do so as your quilt design progresses.

Selecting Fabrics

For the simplest checkerboard, choose two fabrics, a light and a dark or medium dark.

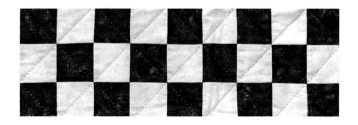

For a design with a little more interest, choose two lights and two medium-dark fabrics, and mix them up a little differently as you see has been done here.

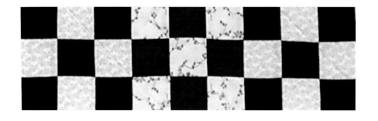

Be a little more random and vary the border still further, as in this version.

You could adjust the contrast to be less defined with light and medium values, or even all light if you don't want to emphasize the inner border as much.

How to Strip Piece

☞ Cut three strips 2½" wide from both the light and dark fabrics (six total).

☞ Join the strips with ¼" seams into two strip-sets:
one Light/Dark/Light
one Dark/Light/Dark

☞ Press the seams towards the darker fabric on both strips. Use a dry iron and press with care to avoid the problem of a hidden fold at the seam. Angle the iron so the point hits the seams straight on to prevent this.

☞ Trim the short end of the strip-sets and cut them into 2½" segments.

☞ Join two segments, one from each strip-set in pairs, then sew the pairs together, chain piecing if you like, and so on and so on until you have your checkerboard border unit the size you want. Make two. Press the seams in alternating directions or all in the same direction.

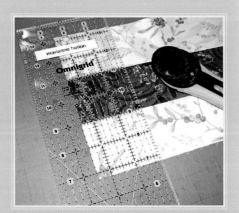

☞ You can make smaller strip-sets with a variety of fabrics or alternate the direction of the dark/light/dark segments for a more random look. The checkerboard is a simple but strong look that works within the scope of many of the quilt designs, and the 2" units make it easy to align the other blocks later on.

☞ Enjoy putting the strip-pieced top and bottom borders on you design wall along with the Log Cabin blocks and move on to the next piece!

There's More Than
One Way to Hand Appliqué

The appliqué components of the quilt are ones where your theme can be nicely showcased while bringing a different technique into the piece. Trying some handwork at this stage of the quilt makes for a change of pace from working on the machine. Appliqué is worth learning because is so versatile—it opens up so many possibilities, enabling the creation of curves and more intricate shapes that are just not possible to do quite the same way by piecing.

Many quilters shy away from appliqué but often get hooked once they try it. Like most things, it becomes easier and faster as you go along. I had limited success with appliqué until I learned the basics from a teacher in Singapore, Brigitte Lee. Her students did fine appliqué and I wanted to know how! Once I get going on a piece of appliqué work, I soon fall into the rhythm and enjoy the gentle pace that handwork provides.

JAPANESE IMPRESSIONS, *detail*

About Appliqué

The word "appliqué" comes from the French verb "appliquér" meaning "to apply." The process of doing appliqué literally has you cutting the fabric in the shape of whatever it is you wish to create and applying it to a background fabric, stitching it down as invisibly as possible. It is possible to create quite elaborate scenes and pictures this way as one can overlap fabrics and impart a more "painterly" feel to a project.

When creating flowers and leaves you can achieve the lovely curves and shapes needed to make them look more natural with appliqué.

PINK VIEW, *detail*

You may be familiar with the intricate two-tone quilts made by Hawaiian quilters, the brightly colored reverse-appliqué molas made by the Cuna Indians of the San Blas region of Panama, and the lovely panels made by the people of Laos with their delicate and closely spaced curlicues in the design. These are all done by some variation of appliqué.

In the United States, the Baltimore Album quilts have no rivals for their magnificence. Ornate floral wreaths, garlands, and baskets of flowers and leaves adorn their surfaces in unabashed abundance, and require skill and competence in the appliqué stitch to be well executed. Nobody, however, is born with a mastery of appliqué, and all these fine stitchers began at the beginning, and so shall we!

Start with a simple heart shape to practice, make four to reinforce what you learn, and then perhaps move on to a snowflake.

Choosing an Appliqué Technique

I have come to prefer two different appliqué techniques and find my students seem to manage best with them.

Needle-turn appliqué requires that the design be drawn onto the *right side* of the piece of fabric being appliquéd. It is basted onto the background to hold it firmly while you stitch around the edge. I much prefer a fine line marker to using a pencil, as a pencil line tends to be fatter and less precise.

The second is a combination of techniques using freezer-paper templates. I iron the template onto the *wrong side* of the fabric and use the edge it provides as the guide to needle-turn the fabric under. Sometimes when using freezer paper, the raw edges are turned under and basted onto the paper first. However, I prefer to simply baste or pin the fabric and freezer paper in place and use the edge of the paper as my guide for where to fold and stitch down the edge as I go. After the piece is stitched in place, I make a small slit from the back in the background layer and remove the paper.

This technique was used on the three flower appliqués in My Garden (page 21) and worked equally well for the stems as for the flowers.

Try both techniques. In the end it is very much a thing of personal preference. Four hearts with their points close together make an easy and attractive block. If you feel ready, try a snowflake. There are also several patterns provided to try, with varying levels of difficulty (pages 91–93). It is even more fun to design your own block.

Supplies and Tools

- Light background fabric
- Darker fabric for the appliqué
- Milliners needles
- Thread to match the fabric of the applied piece. Silk is optional but an excellent choice for invisible stitches.
- ½" appliqué or sequin pins
- Pigma 01 permanent pen (for light fabrics)
- Clover® Fine White Marking Pen (for dark fabrics) or a Sewline® Fabric Pencil
- Freezer paper (optional)
- Plastic template material

This list represents the best tools for the job as I know them. Although perfectly beautiful appliqué can be done using regular pins, needles, and thread, the difference using the silk thread is especially noticeable. Since the thread is that much finer, the use of a milliners needle, which is long and fine, is desirable. You will find you are able to catch just the tiniest edge as you stitch, making for practically invisible stitches. My students always laugh when I show them the tiny half-inch pins, but soon come to love them as the thread doesn't catch on them each time you take a stitch—frustration diminished instantly!

TEAL SAMPLER, *detail*

Cut your background a little larger than you are going to need eventually, but remember it should fit the 2" multiple to work well in the plan. Unfinished 6½" background blocks are good choices. Four can be pieced together to make a 12" (finished) block.

Try piecing the background for the appliqué to add to the overall interest of the block. You'll notice a pieced background on many of the blocks in the quilts (the Koi, for example, on page 55).

Choosing an Appliqué Design

Heart

Because it has both inside and outside points and a nice curve, the heart is the perfect shape to begin with. To cut a good heart is easy. Simply fold a piece of paper in half, then draw half the heart shape, cut it out, and open the paper. (There is also a heart design on page 91.) Try making it about 4"–5" across and a little longer from top to bottom.

Make a template out of rigid plastic template material so you have a firm shape to draw around. Use a 6½" light square for the background. If you do one heart in each method, you will be able to compare the two techniques.

Snowflake Cutout

Try a snowflake—which is essentially Hawaiian-style appliqué—to really get to know your way around points and inside and outside curves. It is fun to draw and cut your own. Try a simple one initially, and increase the complexity if you feel like trying it again. Cutting a pattern is fun—rather like the paper snowflakes we used to cut as, or for, children.

Fold an 11" square of paper in half and fold it in half again. Then make a sharp diagonal fold from corner to corner. Draw a simple design in the manner of the ones you see here, or trace one of the designs provided (pages 91–93). You can make your design relate to your theme, if possible. One for a winter theme could have a real snowflake look; a nature-related theme could have one that looked like a leaf. How about the semblance of a pineapple for a Hawaiian theme, tulips for a Dutch one, daffodils for spring, or thistles for Scotland? Try not to make it too complicated, but also try not to have it look too dumpy and fat.

I suggest just using your paper pattern to draw the snowflake design onto your fabric. It is quite a chore to cut it out in plastic!

Drawing Your Own Design

Find an outline of something with a simple shape that fits your theme. Many of the flowers on the quilts were drawn freehand. These birds were traced from photographs.

Do be bold about trying to draw something. Most of us, myself included, are very reticent about pulling out our drawing skills, believing them to be non-existent. "Oh, I can't draw a straight line," we say. Too true—few of us can!

I surprised myself by sketching the two outermost flowers on MY GARDEN (page 21) and also drew a rendition of an iris I had seen in a very old quilt book. They all came out fine, and so will yours. You may throw away a few attempts, but each try will get better, and the process will start to yield results. It's that old problem of allowing ourselves to play, and to try and try again if necessary, until we get the effect we want.

Cutting Out Your Appliqué Piece

Pin your paper pattern to the right side of the fabric. Trace around the paper template using a Pigma or fine white pen. Remove the paper and cut out the fabric shape with a scant 3⁄16" seam allowance—1⁄4" is just too much!

An alternative method works for a snowflake design. Fold a 12½" x 12½" square of dark or medium-dark fabric in half and in half again, wrong sides together. Open the paper pattern to expose ¼ of the design and pin it to the fabric so the folds correspond. Cut through all the layers at once 3⁄16" beyond the edge of the pattern. Remove the paper pattern. Unfold the fabric and use the Pigma pen or fine white marker to draw a sewing line 3⁄16" inside the cut edge.

BACKYARD BIRDS, *detail*

Needle-Turn Appliqué

One of my favorite ways to appliqué is the needle-turn method. Position the cut-out appliqué piece on the background fabric. Pin, then baste it onto the background ¼" inside the drawn line.

To ensure a smooth edge, use your thumb and forefinger to fold and finger press the edge of the fabric under about ½" to ¾" ahead of your stitching. Fold exactly on the drawn line, pinching a little bit at a time, giving the fabric the "memory" of the fold.

To stitch, thread your needle with thread matching the appliqué piece. Knot it and come up from the underside of the background. Use the needle to smooth the raw edge of the appliqué under, finger pressing as you go. Use the thumb of your non-sewing hand to hold the appliqué against the background,

Catch the very edge of the fold, then insert the needle into the background right next to where the thread came out of the appliqué piece and just to the inside of the fold so that the stitch actually "rolls" the edge under slightly and virtually disappears.

Come up no more than ⅛" further along the line (even closer on a sharp curve or point), catch the very edge of the fold, then down again through the background. Repeat. Use the needle to stroke and smooth the folded edge as you go, so that points don't form.

The thread "travels" on the underside of the background so the stitch shows only as a tiny dot, if at all, on the right side. On the back, the stitches are larger.

On curves, the natural bias that inevitably happens on curved shapes will work in your favor in getting a smooth edge to the shape. You can get away without clipping the edges of an outside curve (convex), but on an inside curve (concave) and especially on a tight curve, you may need to snip the seam allowance just a little bit to achieve a smooth edge. Make the snips quite close but never right to the line.

To do an inside point or "V" such as on the top side of a heart, make one tiny snip into the seam allowance at the point, but not right up to your drawn line. Using your needle, turn under the edge on the "approaching" and "leaving" sides. Then use the needle to create the "V" by "stroking" or "sweeping" underneath the point with a "U" motion, each time trying to define the point a little better. Then stitch it down with even smaller stitches than you have used so far.

To do an outside point, as you will need to do on the bottom of the heart, prepare for the point as you approach it. When you are about an inch away from the point, carefully fold the fabric under straight across the point. Then fold under the approaching edge. Stitch right to the point and fold the leaving side under, doing your best to make the point as sharp as possible. Use your needle to help smooth the way.

Tip Try using a toothpick, perhaps dampened on the point, to help tame unwilling corners and points into submission!

Freezer Paper Plus Needle-Turn Appliqué

When doing the stems and petals on MY GARDEN (page 21), I used freezer paper on the underside of the appliqué along with the needle-turn technique. Having the freezer paper in place provides a sharp edge to use as a guide for turning under the fabric as you stitch. If this is new to you, try it first on a heart, and then try something different.

Draw or trace your appliqué image. Trace each section of the design onto the paper side of the freezer paper without any seam allowance. The paper pieces will be cut to the exact size of the image. If your design is asymmetrical, you need to trace the mirror image of your original drawing. Cut out the shapes on the drawn lines and iron them onto the underside of the appropriate fabric. Cut out the fabric around the freezer paper, leaving 3/16" to turn under.

Arrange the pieces onto the background. If your motif is made of a single piece, such as the bear (page 13), pin and baste it in place. If it has multiple pieces, such as the iris, work the pieces in "layers," first pinning, basting, and stitching the pieces that appear to be on the bottom. Only stitch the edges that will be visible and leave the raw edges of those that will be covered up by successive layers of appliqué. Keep adding the pieces in succession, ending with the top pieces that will cover up all the raw edges, and finish it off.

MY GARDEN, *detail*

My Garden, *detail*

The appliqué stitch is the same as before but the fold is made along the edge of the freezer paper.

I generally wait until after all the pieces have been stitched down to remove the paper. Just make a small slit in the background fabric and pull the paper out, using tweezers if necessary.

After this, it is only left for you to practice to get better at appliqué. I find that the repetitive nature of the snowflake design has made me better at appliqué. Each time I repeat a section it looks vastly improved! If you're aiming for sharp points but not seeing them, well, maybe you can modify your expectations a little and all the points can be made softer, or even the other way around! Remember that flowers are very forgiving designs to work on.

The Skinny on the Skinny!

This is a handy technique for doing flowers and leaves that need very skinny stems:

⬜ Cut a piece of fabric on the true bias 1" wide.

⬜ Fold the strip in half, with the raw edges together and the right-side out.

⬜ Draw a line on the background to indicate where the stem will go—curved or straight.

⬜ Machine stitch the strip to the background, sewing just a tiny bit closer to the raw edge than the fold, following the drawn line.

⬜ Press the folded edge over the raw edge, pin, and hand appliqué it in place.

There is no need to neaten off the edges if they'll be covered by the flower or caught in the seam. You can modify the width by playing around with the cut width, and do your stems thinner or fatter as you like.

The Perfection of Foundation Paper Piecing

It was a long time before I tried paper piecing. I was a competent piecer by hand and by machine, and I could even piece pointy little Mariner's Compass points. Granted, I had only ever pieced one such tour-de force and it was quite difficult! So it was with surprise and delight that I discovered the amazingly accurate world that piecing on a paper foundation opened up to me.

I started, as I often do, without having any clue as to the technique and gradually found through my mistakes the correct way to do it. Once on the right path, I reveled in this back-to-front and upside-down method of making blocks and loved it. It enabled me to make smaller than normal blocks to slot into the small spaces in these quilts to add interest. It is a great way to expand your quilt's theme.

The paper-pieced elk was the perfect addition to the NORTH WOODS quilt where it contributes perfectly to the woods theme as, of course, do the trees.

The dolphins are really having fun in A MARINER'S DREAMS.

The lovely origami cranes are a fitting element in JAPANESE IMPRESSIONS.

At first, foundation piecing seems complicated and is somewhat difficult to visualize, but usually after the first try (and maybe one botched block) the method is easy to master and you will be off and running. I sometimes liken it to patting your head and rubbing your stomach—for to think about placing fabric on the underside, upside down, stitching on the wrong side, etc., etc., sounds rather complicated, but it works better than any other technique for accuracy.

NORTH WOODS, *detail*

A MARINER'S DREAMS, *detail*

JAPANESE IMPRESSIONS, *detail*

I suggest just plunging in with a simple pattern and some fabric and risk making a mistake on your first attempt or two, as there is sometimes no better way to learn how to do something right than to do it wrong! You will soon get the hang of it, I promise.

Selecting a Pattern

There are many wonderful books with loads of patterns available. You may already have some. Many are designed as 4" x 4" blocks, which fit the overall plan for your quilt perfectly. This is where you can really pull the ideas for your theme into the quilt. For now, just try the technique with one of the patterns (pages 91–93) to get familiar with it.

Beginning with a pattern with no more than 10–15 pieces is a good idea, as the blocks start to get more fiddly the more pieces they contain. Some of the patterns like this rooster call for many pieces and look more intricate. They are certainly more time-consuming and just a little more difficult, but never impossible and certainly worth the time.

It is amazing how much of an impact a block this small can have, and that impact can be significantly increased if you use multiples of the same block, or several blocks with the same theme grouped together.

Original design by Marie Lewis

Tools and Supplies

- Paper pattern
- Assorted fabrics—scraps and yardage. Use many different light prints for the background.
- A postcard
- Fabric scissors, a rotary cutter, and mat
- Small clear ruler with grid or an Add-a-Quarter™ quilting tool
- Iron, set on dry, or a flat, finger-pressing tool to "press" without using the iron
- Tweezers—to help remove paper from tight spots

Tips Avoid any fabrics you feel need to be placed in a certain direction.

It is simply not important to worry about straight-of-grain when doing this type of piecing.

Your finished block will be a mirror-image of the foundation pattern, so plan accordingly if it seems to matter.

Foundation Paper Piecing

Preparing the Pattern

Copy or trace the block pattern onto regular copier or tracing paper. If there is not already a ¼" outside seam allowance marked, mark one yourself.

Cut out the block foundation an additional ¼" from the outside seam allowance line. Mark the paper pattern RS (right side—the side with the printed design where you will be stitching) and WS (wrong side—the blank side, although when the fabric is added, it will become the right side of the block!).

Cutting and Placing the First Patch

Cut a piece of fabric large enough to cover area #1. The fabric does not need to be the exact shape of the area, but it must extend at least ¼" beyond the edges. Pin the fabric to the WS—wrong side—of the paper, right side of fabric showing.

I recommend cutting the fabric at least ¾" larger than the overall measurement of the area to be covered. Cutting a shape significantly larger will help you get acquainted with the process and avoid a skimpy cut that does not cover adequately. Once you have the hang of it, you'll get better at gauging how better to cut the fabrics so that you waste less fabric.

Hold the foundation up to the light to be sure the fabric is covering the area adequately.

Trimming the Raw Edge

Working from the RS, position the edge of the postcard along the seam line between areas #1 and #2 and crease the paper back over the postcard.

Trim the exposed edge of the fabric to ¼" using a rotary cutter and a small grid ruler or an Add-a-Quarter tool. Unfold the paper. You'll use the trimmed edge to line up the next patch of fabric.

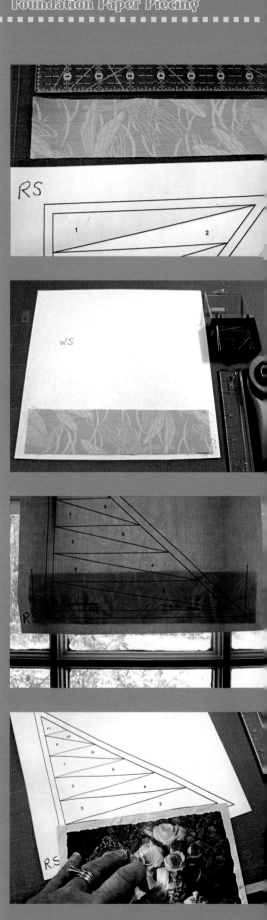

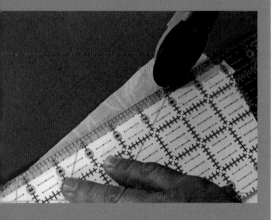

Adding the Second Patch of Fabric

Cut a piece for area #2, large enough to ensure adequate coverage. Working on the WS, align the straight edge of the second patch with the trimmed edge of patch #1, right sides of the fabrics together. Remove the pin and re-pin through both fabrics and the foundation. In time you will be able to hold the new patch in place without pins.

Hold the paper up to the light, looking at it from the RS, each time you place a new patch to be sure you have placed the fabric correctly. Flip over the newly added piece to make sure it covers the area.

Stitching the Patches

Set your machine stitch length very small—1.5–2.0 or 16–18 stitches per inch. This will perforate the paper for easy removal. Stitch from the RS along the seam line between areas #1 and #2. Begin two or three stitches before the outer seam allowance line and finish two or three stitches beyond it.

Pressing the Patch into Place

WS up, press the fabric into place over area #2 with your fingernail, a finger presser tool, or a dry iron. Be sure the fabric covers the space with a healthy ¼" extra all around.

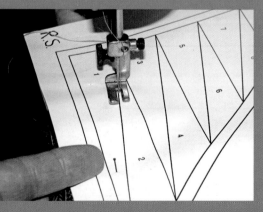

Working from the RS, position the edge of the postcard along the seam line between areas #2 and #3 and crease the paper back over the postcard.

Trim the edge of the fabric to ¼". Unfold the paper.

Working on Subsequent Patches

Cut and place the next patch aligning the raw edge with the previous patch right sides together.

Hold up the block to light to check the placement.

Sew on the seam line.

Press the new patch open.

Fold back the paper and trim the raw edge and you're ready to add the next patch.

Remember, the pieces with outside edges *must* extend beyond the edge of the block pattern and cover the ¼" seam allowance. They will be trimmed neatly at the end.

Notice that if a different fabric is used in each of the patches, including the background, it makes for a more interesting block.

Finishing Up

When all the patches have been added, press with a dry iron on the fabric side. Then flip back to the design side and trim, **making absolutely certain you are trimming on the outer ¼" seam allowance line.**

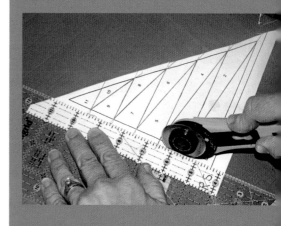

I usually don't remove the paper until the foundation-pieced blocks are sewn into the quilt. Keeping the paper in enables me to piece these blocks together by sewing exactly on the line and matching them together precisely at the corners. For this particular design, you would need to make the second half, a mirror image of the design, and seam the two sections together on the diagonal seam line.

When you are ready to remove the paper you will find it tears out quite easily, as you have sewn with tiny stitches that perforate the paper and make for easy removal. It helps to score along the stitched line with the point of a seam ripper. Occasionally a tweezers may be needed for points that are particularly difficult to reach.

This technique could be done by hand and may make an excellent portable project. Instead of on paper, trace or draw the design onto a lightweight fabric foundation, which is left in permanently.

While initially it might seem a topsy-turvy scheme for piecing, I find most people love the way these blocks turn out, and that it enables a degree of accuracy previously quite difficult to master. So have fun, find the theme blocks available in so many excellent books and magazines, and consider yourself master of a new technical skill in your quilting repertoire.

Designing Your Own Blocks

If you are unable to find something suitable for your theme, you can also draw your own patterns. Now that you are familiar with the technique, you will see what is important in creating a pattern.

For ITALIAN MOSAIC (page 19), Sally drew her own lovely sunflowers and made a row of them for greater emphasis. I drew the spiky sections of the sun that beats down in ...AND A KOOKABURRA IN A GUM TREE (page 20); then used appliqué for the center section; and the curved-seam technique for the outer regions. Three techniques in one block!

...AND A KOOKABURRA IN A GUM TREE, *detail*

Perfect Curved Seams:
Not Nearly as Scary as You Thought They Would Be!

We ALL want perfect curves! Most of us don't get them where we want them, but you can get them here! This simple little block is sometimes an intimidating one, one quilters often put off trying. But it's really a cinch. You will be amazed at how proficient you will become if you follow the steps and try one or two.

Making the Templates

Template Supplies

- One sheet of gridded template plastic
- A compass
- An ultra-fine point permanent marker
- Scissors—the pair you keep for cutting paper and plastic only!

Instructions for Drafting a 4" Block

The templates can be used for both hand and machine piecing as the stitching is much the same for both.

Inch-line increments on gridded template plastic are usually bold, so a 4" square will be easy to see. I usually double-check with a ruler to be sure the measurements are exact. Start by marking a dot at each of the four corners of a 4" square. You can leave the four outside lines of the square unmarked, unless you feel more comfortable drawing them in. You will cut the templates later on the exact grid lines indicated by the dots.

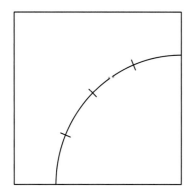

Draw registration marks first.

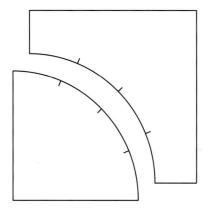

Then cut the templates apart.

Next, make sure your compass has a good sharp pencil or piece of lead in it. A good proportion for this curved seam is ¾ of the length of the side. So set your compass at 3". Recalling your high school geometry class, place the point of the compass on one corner dot and "describe an arc" between the two adjacent sides of the square as shown.

Check the accuracy of your lines and the dimensions of your square. Draw three registration marks across the curve as shown. Mark each piece "this side up." You need to place the templates consistently facing up as you trace or draw around them onto fabric so the registration marks will line up accurately and position the fabrics for a perfect curve.

Add arrows showing the grain line, although in this case it is obvious. Placing the straight edge of the template along the straight of grain will ensure that the curve will fall on the maximum bias. This makes piecing the curved seam a cinch, as the bias works for you all the way.

Next, cut the two template pieces apart along the curve. It seems to work best to hold the scissors straight and to turn the plastic as you cut, rather than to try to cut around the curve. Begin with the scissors wide open and make the cut with only one or two closures of the scissors. Then cut around the sides of the two templates.

Selecting Fabrics

Try not to be too choosy about the fabrics. Just go for some value contrast.

If you take a look at the quilts in the book you will see various possibilities for placing the darks, mediums, and lights. The circles in many of the quilts have a rather random feel. Some have a more ordered placement of lights and darks to follow the pattern in the blocks that balance the circles at the opposite corner of the quilts.

This technique was used to create the pagoda in JAPANESE IMPRESSIONS (page 31) but the circles have been defined very differently.

LEFT: JAPANESE IMPRESSIONS, *detail*

Preparing to Make Circle Blocks

You will need:

- A selection of light, medium, and darker fabrics
- A sheet of emery cloth
- A very sharp pencil or Pigma pen
- Pins
- Neutral thread
- Fabric scissors

Select two contrasting fabrics. Using a sheet of emery cloth to stabilize the fabric, place one fabric wrong-side up, and place one of the templates "this-side up" on the fabric, paying attention to the straight of grain. Hold the template down firmly with your fingers at the edge. First mark a dot at each corner of the template. These will be the start and finish points for each seam. Then draw around the shape. Transfer the registration marks. Draw around the second template on the contrasting fabric.

Cut out the pieces ¼" beyond the drawn line. Practice "eye-balling" the amount and cutting a smooth and consistent seam.

Pinning the Pieces

The pinning is the most important step to follow carefully to line up the seams perfectly for accurate stitching. Use the same technique whether you are hand or machine stitching.

Lay the pieces with their curves together, overlapping them by half an inch to accommodate the seam allowances, and they'll fit perfectly. Take the convex, three-sided **"pie wedge"** piece, and flip it over on top of the concave, five-sided **"bite-out"** piece, **right sides together,** so that the center registration marks line up. The curves will be going in completely opposite directions when you do so, but all is well!

Success lies in the dots and the registration marks when it comes to curved seams, and you are going to go "dot to dot."

Pin the two pieces together at the center registration marks. Pierce the mark on the "pie" piece precisely on the seam line with a pin. Find the mark on the "bite" piece and poke the pin through it, too. **Push the two fabrics together on the shaft of the pin,** then poke the pin back through the top fabric, ⅛" from the line.

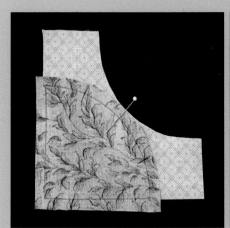 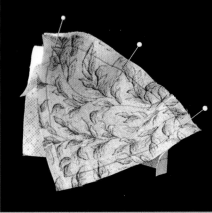 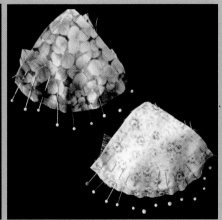

It looks as though the curves will never line up, but have faith, they will! Ignoring the curve, swing the pie piece around until the straight side aligns with the short straight side of the bite piece. Matching the dots in the same way, pin so that you keep the straight edges aligned! Now do exactly the same with the other side.

OK. That was the tricky part. Now pin the pieces together at the remaining two registration marks *very accurately*. The pins should all be pointing inward. There will now be five pins in place and you need only put one or two more in each of the four spaces between the pins. Sometimes I find I want do more pinning—two pins in each space works well as it positions them about ½" apart. Stretch the fabrics a bit to get the pins in right. Don't be afraid to do this. Stretching will really help distribute the fullness evenly and will eliminate folds; the seam will lie flat and even.

If you have followed this lengthy description for what is really much less complicated a procedure than it sounds, you are now poised to sew a simple seam and enjoy the results.

Sewing a Curve by Hand

Your sewing will be on the lines only and not extend into the seam allowances. You'll stitch in the same way that you hand stitch a straight seam (pages 43–44).

Thread a needle with neutral thread. Hold the piece with the seam and pins toward you. Starting ⅜" into the seam, stitch along on the seam line toward the dot, taking 4–5 tiny running stitches absolutely no larger than a scant ⅛" long. Remove the pin and stitch through the dot, then pivot and stitch to the dot at the other end of the seam with the same little stitches. Remove the pin, stitch through the dot, turn the work around again, and sew back into the seam for four or five stitches. You can take the pins out as you go or when you finish, if they aren't a nuisance or don't catch the thread as you sew.

Stretch the seam somewhat as you sew. The bias will recover and the seam will be the better for your having done so. Check as you go along that the stitching line does indeed fall on the pencil line on both fabrics. If it is not happening, probably the pinning wasn't what it should have been. Just try again. Doing it wrong once is usually the best way to learn the right way!

Use the blocking technique (pages 45–46) and pin down each of the corners on an accurate ironing grid, pressing with a dry iron. Or you can try my current preferred technique of joining all the circle blocks in their final arrangement before blocking them. Because of the piecing technique you have used, the seams are not committed to lie in any particular direction; you can choose later how you would like them to lie to reduce the bulk at the seam intersections. The curved seam, interestingly, will be happy lying in either direction.

Joining the Blocks

Once you have decided on the arrangement of your blocks, join them following the same pointers for accurate hand stitching as given for the curves. Stitch through the base of the seam allowances at the dots, leaving the seam allowances free. (See the hand-piecing instructions on page 42 for a refresher on handling the seam allowances.)

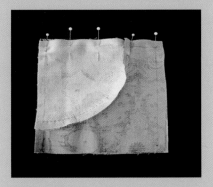

Here is a seam pinned and ready for stitching by hand.

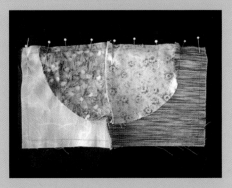

This is the pinning setup for joining multiple blocks together.

Here is the back of a unit stitched together and ready for pressing.

This last picture details the special things about piecing with this technique. The seam intersections open up to press in any direction you want, thus reducing the bulk, and you get an accurate outcome.

Curved seams lend themselves to many creative design ideas—grape-vines, temples, moons...what next?

Sewing a Curve by Machine

Almost everything that applies to hand stitching applies if you are going to piece by machine, so do read through the directions for hand stitching (pages 43–44). After pinning as discussed (page 71), you can stitch in one of two ways.

Stitch from Dot to Dot

Stitch from a point ¼" into the seam back toward the dot. With the needle down, raise the presser foot and gently pivot the work 180 degrees, then sew along the full length of the seam to the dot, stretching as you go, with the bulk of the piece to the left of the presser foot. Pivot the work again at the dot and take a couple of stitches into the seam. This is the truly precise way to piece accurately, and it will give you the same flexibility as in hand piecing to determine which way your seams will lie when you block and press.

Stitch from Raw Edge to Raw Edge

Alternatively, pin as before but add a pin within the seam allowance to keep the seams aligned, ensuring no distortion. Stitch from raw edge to raw edge, stretching the seam as you sew. You can sew over the pins, unless your machine objects horribly. With good quality fine pins most machines are quite tolerant of this exercise.

Block and press each curved seam with a dry iron before proceeding to the next step, alternately pressing toward and away from the quarter-circle patch. Then when you join the blocks, the seams will lie in opposite directions to reduce bulk. The biggest difference when piecing by machine this way is that you stitch the seam allowances down when you join the blocks.

I usually save final pressing until the blocks are joined. I feel the result is more accurate. I block the unit wrong-side up (page 45), then press from the right side.

The Kaleidoscope Block:
No Curved Seams—Just an Illusion!

The Kaleidoscope is probably the trickiest of the designs offered here but is by far and away one of the most interesting patterns. The intrigue is twofold. The first lies in the variations created by the placement of light and dark fabrics. It is possible to create a group of interlocking compass-like shapes or fractured circles, depending on where you position the values.

The second and even more interesting feature is the illusion of circles or curves that develops, when all you have worked with are straight lines and rigid angles!

A 6" block works well in the sampler. A small version with four Kaleidoscope blocks gives you a completed 12" unit. A larger version with nine blocks gives you a completed 18" unit and is something of a challenge; but my students always say they are glad they made the effort, as the outcome is spectacular.

The curves show up better on the larger version and it has more scope for making a center compass design more apparent, but it can sometimes overpower a small quilt. That, however, did not stop me from putting the larger version into MY GARDEN (page 21). The smaller one is also very attractive and serves the purpose well.

In deciding which version to make, it is especially helpful to have completed some of the other blocks so you can see how they all start to fit together. If you make a small set and a large set of *paper* Kaleidoscope blocks, you will get a good sense of their relationship to the other blocks before you begin.

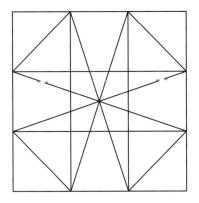

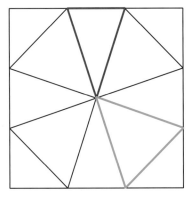

Different size wedges can be confusing.

IMAGINING SOMETHING BEAUTIFUL, *51" x 63". Made by Jean-Marie Gard, Redmond, WA.*

Drafting the Kaleidoscope Block

I have included a template pattern for the two triangle shapes needed to make the block (page 92), but I think it is valuable to draft the Kaleidoscope yourself to really understand how it works.

If you look at the basic block, at first it appears that it is drafted by dividing a block as one would for a nine-patch, but the wedge-shaped triangles end up being two different sizes. There is huge potential for confusion in keeping the different size patches separated.

It is preferable to draft the block so that the wedge-shaped triangles are of equal size, and all it takes is simple geometry—a compass and ruler are the only tools you need. This method is easy and straightforward and it is fun to have a reason to pick up and play with tools many of us haven't used since we were in high school.

Supplies Needed

- Accurate ¼" graph paper
- Gridded template plastic
- Compass
- Ruler
- Pencil

Drawing on graph paper first is a good idea to get the steps right. It is not necessary to draw the whole block on the template plastic. Once you have done it on paper, you will know which portion you need to draw on the template material.

Drafting

- Draw an accurate 6" x 6" square on graph paper.

- Mark the exact center with a dot. Set the compass point at a corner with the pencil point on the center dot. Describe an arc—that high school geometry is coming back now—through the center dot that intersects the two adjacent sides.

- Repeat at the other three corners. The four arcs should meet in the center of the block.

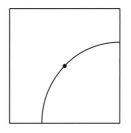 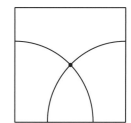

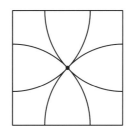 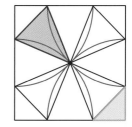

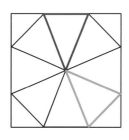

Draw lines connecting the points as shown to create the two triangles needed for this block.

The wedge-shaped triangles are of equal size. You now have the lines in place to make the only two templates needed to make the whole Kaleidoscope pattern. That was easy, wasn't it?

You need only to mark out one corner of the block on your template plastic, as shown. Use a very fine permanent marker to mark the lines so there is no uncertainty as to where to cut. A fat line will lessen the accuracy of the template. Every fraction of an inch off will add up and distort the finished block.

When you are certain that the templates are drawn accurately, cut them out exactly on the drawn lines with scissors (which I prefer) or a rotary cutter.

Add grain lines as shown. Mark each template with your initials, its name, and the size block it is for.

Drafted Kaleidoscope block with same size wedges.

Playing with Paper

With most of the other blocks, I have encouraged you to plunge in with fabric, but here I suggest you play a little with paper and pencils for a while. These blank diagrams of both four blocks and nine blocks (page 78) are provided for you to copy and shade in trying different ways.

I prefer working solely in pencil for this exercise. If you prefer, do it in color. You don't need to represent each of your fabrics with a particular color; it is much more important that you differentiate the values.

Try several arrangements using the value difference to place emphasis on different areas and you will produce remarkably different designs. Study the different Kaleidoscope designs in the book and try to replicate one of them on paper.

NORTH WOODS, *53" x 66". Made by Carol Ballou, Sudbury, MA.*

Doak, Hiney, McCloskey, Smith & Milligan, and *Quilters Newsletter* pattern credits page 94

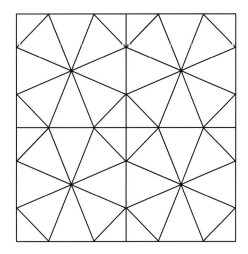

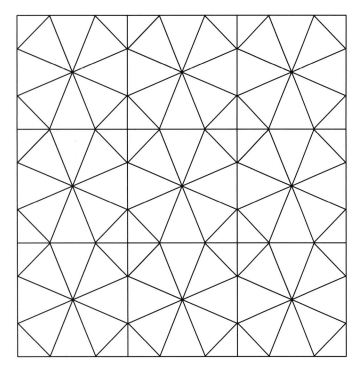

The effect you're seeking is one where the emphasized design floats upon the light colored background. Remember, the goal within this style of quilt is to unite the entire quilt by using background fabrics with similar value, so it is important to keep the outer edges of the Kaleidoscope unit light, so that it blends with its neighbor.

Working with fabric

Once you have played on paper, the best way to really get the Kaleidoscope right is to work with the fabric pieces on a design wall, or on a piece of flannel or felt about 30" square—essentially a portable design wall.

The Kaleidoscope block affords you a chance to use a big variety of fabrics. Cut a number of the large triangles in dark, medium, and light fabric following the same procedure for marking the seam lines with dots and Xs and cutting as before (pages 76–77). In planning the layout, stand back and consider the placement of each patch for its value and overall impact. I love the freedom this block gives you to create.

When you have the definition of your design in place, you can cut the small triangles, most of which usually end up being lights. There is still room for tweaking and rearranging to get the design just right.

The six variations of the Kaleidoscope block shown opposite use exactly the same set of fabrics.

Rearranging is a really fine exercise as it illustrates the impact that value has in the quilt blocks. If you use a digital camera to photograph your variations, you'll find it interesting to see them alongside each other. You can print them

A very simple variation—not too exciting.

The circular effect is starting to show.

More changes and the compass becomes evident.

Even more moves and the whole effect changes to a tighter shape. The compass stays, but there are a few more elements inside the center.

The center is lightened up somewhat, and a different shape appears.

There are some elements reaching outward.

up in color for good effect, and if you do so in black and white you will have a different look at the value contrast—one not influenced by color.

Once you are happy with the arrangement, it's sew time!

Keeping the Pieces in Order

Because each of the blocks within the arrangement is different, it is important to have a strategy to keep the pieces organized. It is oh so very easy to pick up a few pieces, take them to the machine, sew the wrong edges together, and only discover the glitch later!

First (and this has helped me on many an occasion when I lost track of where I was), take a photo to refer to if something gets confusing or out of place. Next, one by one, lift the pieces of each block onto a sheet of paper and pin them in place. If the phone rings, or the wind blows, or the cat decides to have a nap on the arrangement, you're covered!

Be sure to note on the paper the correct orientation of the block. This will help when it comes time to sew on the corner triangles. You can take this paper with you to the machine, pinning each set of pieces back onto the paper as it is sewn or simply place your portable design wall next to your machine. Remove the pieces, sew them together, and put them back to ensure that you keep them in their correct place.

How to Piece a Kaleidoscope Block and Stay Sane

You can sew this block by hand or machine. Picking up one pair of center triangles at a time, use the dot-to-dot piecing method (page 74), pin, and sew them. Finger press each seam to one side. The seams all need to lie in the same direction. Put them back in position, join the next two, and so on. Then join the pairs into sets of four. Use the dots to pin carefully. I always put a third pin between the dots, matching the seam lines of the two pieces. You can add the corner triangles as you go along or add them after the center octagon is sewn together. Either way works.

Please note, I still haven't suggested pressing the seams.

The Trickiest Seam of All: Bringing All Eight Points Together—Demystified

Bring the points of your 2 four-triangle (half-octagon) units together in the center and find the visible dots. The seams will butt together beautifully because you have all the seam allowances following each other around in the same direction, right? If you don't, make it happen!

Ease the two halves together and pierce a pin through the dots, making sure they don't slide away from each other. You may want to pin across the dot, keeping the points together very carefully. Pin at the dots at the outside edges and along the seam with perpendicular pins, then have a go at the seam.

At this point, if I am machine piecing, I sew right across the center seam. Only with a bit of trial and error will you know whether your pinning is working and the points are coming out (almost) perfectly. Even after all the practice I still find times that I just haven't got it right. Usually it is a fairly simple fix, and sometimes it is too small a mismatch to worry about.

Don't forget to add the four corner triangles if you haven't yet. Following the dots makes it an easy piecing job.

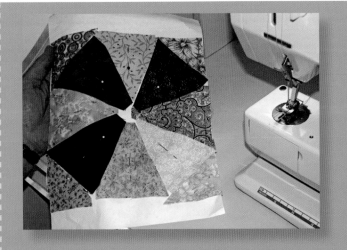

You can sew this block by hand or machine. Pinning the pieces to a sheet of paper will help keep them in order for piecing.

Perfect Pinwheel

Now, if you have sewn the block by hand or by machine using the dot-to-dot method (page 74), when you lay the block flat, and you finger press all the seams in the same direction, the center will open up and a tiny little pinwheel will appear. When pressed, all the bulk of those many seams coming together will be as evenly distributed as possible, making for a very flat intersection of eight seams!

If, however, you have sewn through the seam allowances by machine, you need to do a little unsewing for the seams to lie flat. Fold the block in half along the final seam. Look for the vertical stitches at the center seam. Undo the two or three stitches of that seam that lie within the seam allowance seam on both sides of the piece. (Read that again if it didn't make sense!) Open out the piece, and lay it flat. Press the seams so that they are all going in the same direction, and the little pinwheel will appear,

Once you have worked your way through the nine (or four) Kaleidoscope blocks, you will be a pro. After blocking the individual blocks, it's a cinch to piece them together, again matching the dots at each intersection. Join the blocks in rows, then sew the rows together. If you did a good job blocking each separate block, the pressing will be minimal at this stage. Work to keep the seams straight as you go, pinning them along a line on your ironing surface grid cloth as you prepare to press them.

And that is the wrap on one of the hardest blocks of all. You should feel so proud for it is not an easy one to do.

If the points aren't perfect please don't fret, for once it is all in the mix, these little inaccuracies fade into the zone of non-importance. Glaring errors are something else, but I always remind my students that as you work with it, you are looking at it about one foot away. You need to get a little more distance from it to see it well. I say, strive for accuracy, then fix it, fudge it, and forget it!

Undoing these stitches allows the seam to open up and lie flat.

Super Accurate
Half-Square Triangles

This is a neat technique you may have come across before. If not, it's a really good one to know. By "neat" I really do mean tidy, as it is so crisp and accurate. It is simple and efficient, and enables you to make perfect units, any size you want to. What's not to love about that?

In the quilts in this book, the technique has been used most often to make the Tree of Life block, but is adaptable to any situation that might require accurate half-square triangles. It works for making filler strips, borders, blocks, and parts of blocks. Even if you don't have a plan for them yet, make some to try out the technique and see what ideas may come to you

Tools and Materials

- Two contrasting fabrics
- A very sharp pencil
- A piece of emery cloth or very fine sand-paper
- A ruler with very accurate grid markings

Tip If you draw a grid of 2⅞" squares to try this technique, you will have a set of 2" (finished) half-square triangles to use as fillers.

Making Half-Square Triangles

- Decide how many blocks you need.

- Draw a grid with half that many squares on the wrong side of the lighter-colored fabric. The squares should be the finished size you want plus ⅞" to provide enough for the seam allowance. Place the fabric on a sheet of emery cloth or fine sandpaper to stabilize it. Each square you draw will produce two half-square triangle units. So for instance, a 3 x 4 grid with 12 squares will yield 24 half-square triangles.

- Draw a diagonal line from corner to corner of the squares as shown on page 83. If you want, draw a sewing line ¼" on both sides of the diagonal lines. Otherwise, you can use your machine foot and settings to achieve a ¼" seam.

- Place the two fabrics right sides together and pin adequately to keep them from shifting.

- Stitch a ¼" seam on both sides of the diagonal lines. Sew in one direction on one side of the line and in the opposite direction on the other to minimize any pulling on the seam.

You can stitch a continuous line, but it will require a bit of "unsewing" later at the tips, so I prefer to stop at the intersections with the needle up and lift the presser foot over the little points of the adjacent block, then carry on sewing the next piece. No backstitching necessary.

Now for the best part. Take out any pins, and place the piece on a cutting mat. With the rotary cutter and ruler, **slice through the solid lines**, separating the squares from one another. Now slice through the diagonal line of each square, and there it is—a perfect half-square triangle with ¼" seams. Go ahead and measure to make sure.

This is a neat technique you may have come across before.

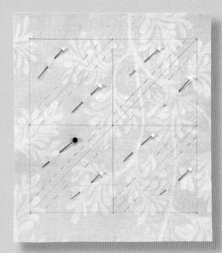

EVERYTHING'S COMING UP ROSES, *detail*

The GridMap Revisited

Well, if you have come this far, I applaud and thank you for sticking with it. This quilt requires a lot of work, and I appreciate your dedication to the task.

Perhaps you have been planning all along where things will sit in relationship to one another, or maybe that was too much to think about at once and you have been stitching away, wondering how all these disparate pieces are going to magically become one!

The first thing you need is your GridMap and all your blocks rendered in pencil on paper (pages 27–33). They are scaled down, correctly proportioned, have no seams, and will help you work out the design. You want to find the balance and best layout possible in small scale first before working with the real thing.

The second thing is to have a design wall to work on to view the stitched pieces (page 25). Using your GridMap as a starting point, you can move the paper blocks around to try them out in relationship to one another in different places, then do the same with the fabric blocks and stand back to assess the way they look.

As you move things around, you will find there are spaces between the elements, and you will need to tighten up the design with small filler strips and block elements (page 87). If a block falls short on size, add a narrow light-colored strip to bring it up to a size compatible with the 4" plan. Or, there may be a section that could really use a set of small blocks in keeping with your theme.

As you tighten the design and close up the gaps, a piecing order will emerge. You'll notice components that can be stitched into larger units, which can then be stitched together into even larger units, and eventually into a whole piece, needing only borders and corner blocks to complete the top.

See page 85 for the PINK VIEW piecing plan before the borders were added.

The block sizes, some 4", 6", 8" 12", and 18", add up to the 42" checkerboard inner border. It makes for an excellent means of keeping the sizes in line with what you want them to be.

PINK VIEW, *50" x 62". Made by Janice*
Carvalho, Stow, MA.

Doak, Fons & Porter, and Rolfe pattern credits page 94

Checkerboard 42" x 6"				

	Appliqué 4" x 4"	4" x 4"	4" x 4"	Appliqué 8" x 10"	Appliqué 4" x 18"
Kaleidoscope 18" x 18"	Filler strip 12" x 2"				
	Appliqué 12" x 12"			FPP 8" x 8"	

FPP 4" x 4"	Curved Seams 8" x 8"	FPP 4" x 4"	FPP 4" x 4"	Tree of Life 12" x 12"	Basket 6" x 6"	FPP 4" x 4"
FPP 4" x 4"		Circle 8" x 8"				FPP 4" x 4"
FPP 4" x 4"	FPP 4" x 4"	FPP 4" x 4"			Basket 6" x 6"	FPP 4" x 4"

FPP 4" x 4"	Log Cabin 12" x 12"	Appliqué 8" x 12"	Basket 6" x 6"	FPP Star 12" x 12"
FPP 4" x 4"				
FPP 4" x 4"			Basket 6" x 6"	

Checkerboard 42" x 6"				

Checkerboard 34" x 6"			

FPP 4" x 4"	Log Cabin 12" x 12"	Appliqué 6" x 10"	Curved Seams 8" x 8"	FPP 4" x 4"
FPP 4" x 4"				FPP 4" x 4"
Appliqué 4" x 14"			Curved Seams 8" x 8"	FPP 4" x 4"
	Kaleidoscope 18" x 18"			FPP 4" x 4"
			Curved Seams 8" x 8"	Appliqué 4" x 14"
FPP 4" x 4"			FPP 4" x 4" / Filler 4" x 2"	
FPP 4" x 4"			Filler 4" x 2" / FPP 4" x 4"	

Checkerboard 34" x 6"			

RIGHT: *My Garden, 45" x 53". Made by the author, also
shown on page 21 and the cover.*

MY GARDEN was assembled as follows:

This time the units were assembled in vertical
strip units. The only additional fillers needed were
the little pieces above and below each robin.

Keep working with your GridMap and the
design surface, adding or subtracting pieces as
needed, until the design meets your satisfaction.
You will know when the time is right to call it a
day and to commit to the sewing machine.

Davis & Shiffer and Doak pattern
credits page 94

Here is the piecing plan for JOYFUL LEARNING.

Because the blocks were made carefully to dimensions that were multiples and divisions of 4", it was easy to join the pieces into units. Those units were then joined into strips, which were then seamed into a whole.

Sometimes there are areas that will require some creative seaming to make things fit. You may need a filler piece to solve the puzzle or just some careful work to fit it all together.

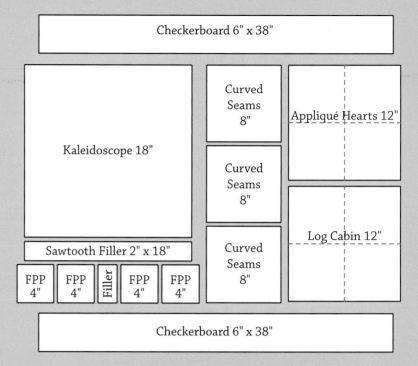

| Checkerboard 6" x 38" |
Kaleidoscope 18"	Curved Seams 8"	Appliqué Hearts 12"
	Curved Seams 8"	
Sawtooth Filler 2" x 18"		Log Cabin 12"
FPP 4"	FPP 4"	Filler	FPP 4"	FPP 4"	Curved Seams 8"	
Checkerboard 6" x 38"

Doak pattern credits page 94

JOYFUL LEARNING, *50" x 48". Made by Bobbi Fisher, Sudbury, MA.*

Simply Dynamic Sampler Quilts ⚓ Marianne L. Hatton

Filling in the Gaps:
Choosing Corner Blocks and Selecting Borders

Filler Strips and Units

After you have worked out your design using the GridMap, you may need to do a little more work filling in some holes or spaces that show up when you arrange the major components of your quilt. There are so many options for filling small spaces including strips of background fabric for narrow gaps, or small pieced strips or blocks. Since these areas are probably going to be small and narrow, you could choose from little borders such as Flying Geese or Sawtooth borders, single or double checkerboards.

There are many little blocks to choose from—Pinwheels, solo Flying Geese blocks, or a host of other little ones whose names I don't even know. It is a cinch to draw and draft these little blocks to fill in the holes in the quilt layout. They can form the basis of larger blocks, or stand on their own. If you piece them in low-contrast background colors to blend, they will be more interesting to look at. Choose whatever piecing technique you would like to use to make them.

Once you have filled all the spaces, you will be ready to stitch your quilt together.

Accurate piecing is a skill that will develop as you progress. It is important to be as precise

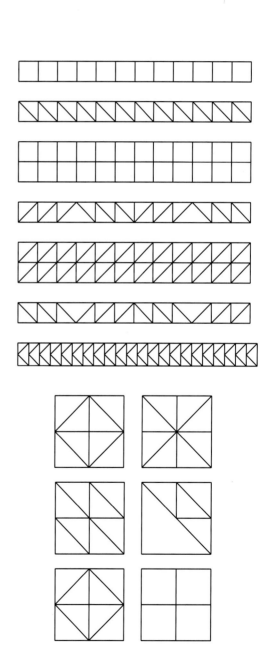

Doak and Hiney pattern credits page 94

EVERYTHING'S COMING UP ROSES, *51" x 66". Made by Terry Cordo, Sudbury, MA.*

as is possible for the satisfaction you will derive from a job well done. Overlook small inaccuracies. If, when you stand back from a piece, a problem is not a glaring mistake, I don't think it should be pulled out.

Follow your GridMap to join the components. **You may need to do some fine-tuning and tweaking** on some of the seams to get things to fit perfectly. It is best to make the adjustments over several seams so as not to be noticeable.

Magic happens when you sew the individual components together. Somehow although one knows intellectually that it should work, it is only when the seams finally get sewn and the raw edges disappear that the piece takes on a special quality and dignified appearance that still thrills me after all these years.

Corner Blocks

Corners don't necessarily have to have any special treatment, but are certainly eye-catching when they do. You can reinforce your theme by choosing a design for the corners that ties in to a central part of the design. In PEACE OF HEAVEN, a gorgeous star extends the celestial theme into the corners of the quilt. Many different fabrics were used, and choosing the background for the first border allowed the stars to blend smoothly into the border.

Davis & Shiffer, Doak, Lenz, and Maddocks pattern credits page 94

LEFT: PEACE OF HEAVEN, *53" x 53". Made by Frances Sharp, Sudbury, MA.*

For COOL AND SHADY (page 32) I made my own paper-pieced pattern for the palm leaf. Different fabrics were used for each pointy piece to continue the interest into the corners. An eight-pointed star was used in the corners of NORTH WOODS (page 77), tying in well with the large, wintry sun, which is also an eight-pointed design. Different fabrics were used in each star point.

COOL AND SHADY, *detail*

It works well to draw a first border fabric into the corner blocks. You can see this in all three of these quilts.

Even though at this point you may just want to get on with the business of finishing up, it seems worth taking a little more time to add some pizzazz to the corners which are often a neglected area on a quilt, but offer an opportunity for a little more design input.

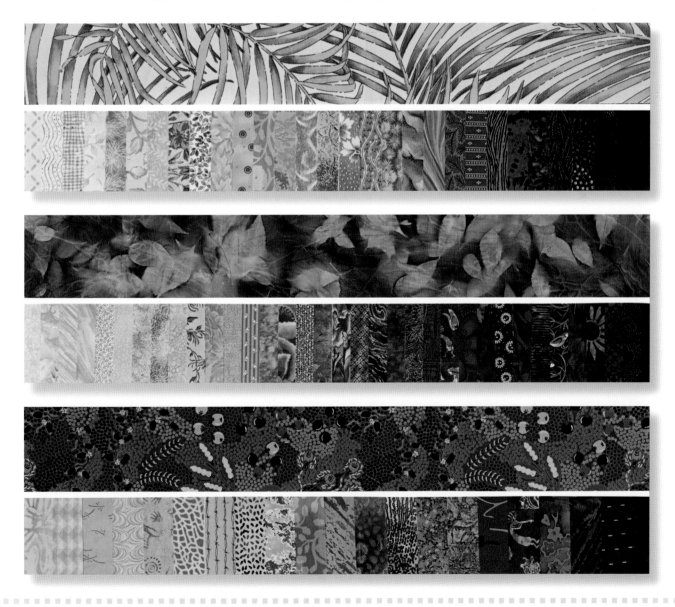

Choosing Border Fabric

JAPANESE IMPRESSIONS, *detail*

You may have begun the quilt with a border in mind, or you may only now be looking for suitable fabrics. It requires an audition to find the right fabric to round out the quilt. A good border should harmoniously tie the components of the quilt together but not overwhelm nor be overwhelmed! The border fabrics shown on page 89 drove the selection of fabrics for possible quilts. The fabrics are ones that blend well and tie in with the border fabrics. The borders on the two quilts shown on this page were chosen after the center sections were completely assembled.

If you are choosing the border after putting the quilt together, you will probably find that there will be more than one good choice of fabrics. The border is a significant part of the quilt and has a lot to say regarding the feel of the quilt. Ask opinions, and go with what makes you happy and seems a fitting frame for the quilt.

You may choose to do the border in two parts as seen in most of the quilts. Some even have a third fabric, a very tiny accent strip. Take a close look at JAPANESE IMPRESSIONS and ITALIAN MOSAIC as examples. That tiny strip of fabric can perk up a border in need of something to accent it.

BELOW: ITALIAN MOSAIC, *detail*

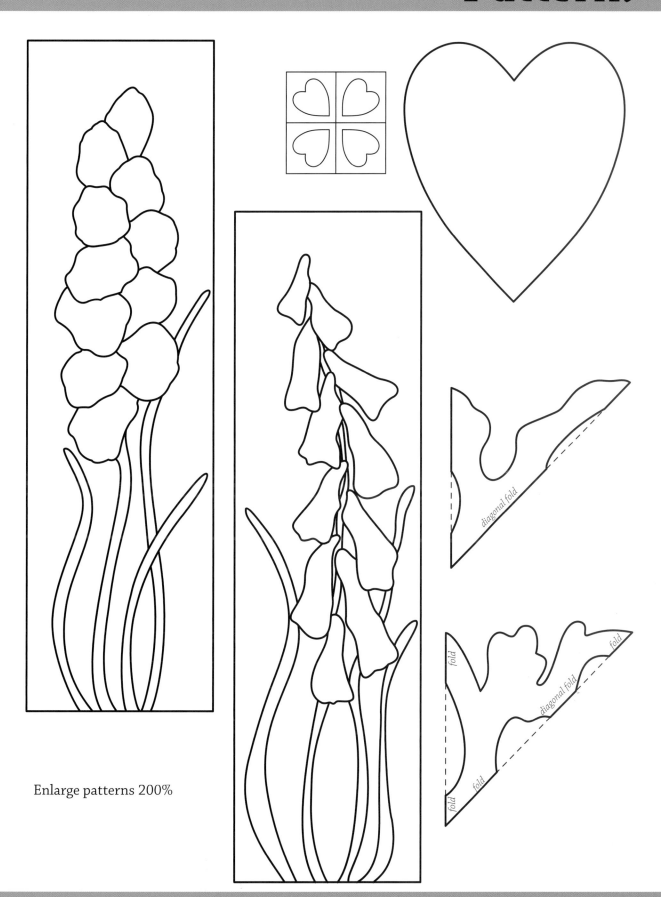

Enlarge patterns 200%

Enlarge patterns 200%

Original pattern by Sally Cameron

center

Original pattern by Cynthia Ross Lauer

Enlarge patterns 200%

fold

fold

diagonal fold

diagonal fold

Books

101 Foundation Pieced Quilt Blocks by Linda Causee. Asn Pub, 1996. Used by permission American School of Needlework/DRG, 306 E. Parr Rd. Berne, IN 46711
Star of Bethlehem, pages 5 and 33
heart, page 76

Quilting Made Easy: More Than 150 Patterns and Inspiring Ideas for Creating Beautiful Quilt Blocks by Jodie Davis and Linda Hampton Schiffer. Friedman/Fairfax Publishing, 1998.
braided heart & lovebird, page 21
Interlaced Star, page 88

Easy Machine Paper Piecing by Carol Doak, That Patchwork Place, 1994.
F10, H1, H2, H3, page 85
H2, page 86
H3, F8, T2, T3, page 30
T2, F7, F8, F10, page 32
H7, H2, H3, F10, page 21
P4, page 33
T1, T2, T3, P6, page 18
T8, T11, T12, H3, F10, page 26
T1, T2, pages 76 and 77
T5, T6, page 5
F7, F10, F14, T11, page 88
F8, T9, page 18

Easy Paper-Pieced Miniatures by Carol Doak, Martingale & Company, Inc., 1998.
mini hearts, page 26

Easy Mix & Match Machine Paper-Piecing by Carol Doak, Martingale & Company, Inc., 1995.
F41, page 30

Easy Paper Pieced Keepsake Quilts by Carol Doak, That Patchwork Place, 1995.
F31, T10, T11, T12, T13 page 30
T9, T10, T11, page 32
T9, page 18, 26, and 86
P25 (adapted) page 33

Quilter's Complete Guide by Marianne Fons and Liz Porter, Oxmoor House, 2001.
Hawaiian Breadfruit page 18, 26, 76, and 85

Beautiful Foundation-Pieced Quilt Blocks by Mary Jo Hiney, Sterling, 2000.
elk, pages 8, 13, 63, and 77
cabbage rose, page 88
kimono, page 31
cranes, pages 31 and 63
flower spray, small stars, page 20

Mariner's Compass Quilts: New Directions by Judy Mathieson, Watson-Guptill Publications, 1995.
Mariner's Compass, page 76

Feathered Star Quilts by Marsha McCloskey, That Patchwork Place, 1987.
Feathered Star, page 77

Welcome to My Cabin by Nancy Smith and Lynda Milligan, Possibilities/Great American Quilt Factory, 2003.
bear, page 13 and 77
cabin, page 77

A Quilter's Ark: More Than 50 Designs for Foundation Piecing by Margaret Rolfe, That Patchwork Place, 1997.
hummingbird & butterflies, page 85
kangaroo & koala, page 33
dolphins, pages 14, 41, and 63
koala, kookaburra, emu, kangaroo, wombat, cockatoo, penguin, page 20
owl, page 18
blue jay, page 26

Quilters Newsletter, May 1984, McKim Kaleidoscope, page 41; November 1991

Web Sites

The Quilter's Cache/Marcia Hohn
www.quilterscache.com

Ula's Quilt Page/Ula Lenz
www.lenzula.com
Shadowstar, page 88

Piece by Number: Paper Piecing Patterns for Quilters/
Beth Maddocks
www.piecebynumber.com
SunRays, page 88

All Crafts
www.allcrafts.net
crocus and daffodil, page 76

Meet
Marianne L. Hatton

PHOTO: Bruce Lucier

I can barely recall a time when I didn't sew. Like many of us, I sewed clothes from a young age and dressed Barbie dolls with garments requiring those tiny eighth-inch buttons and half-inch zippers! It seemed right and proper then that I became a high school home economics teacher so I could sew some more. I have been making quilts for the past 30 years or so, and have taught quiltmaking for at least 20 of those years in adult education settings, privately, and in quilt stores. I owned The Uncommon Thread, a small fabric import business specializing in importing hand-dyed fabrics from South Africa, for about five years, but gave it up to focus more on teaching.

Students in my studio classes range from beginners through experienced quilters. I enjoy

every opportunity to teach—sharing a skill that fosters creativity, brings such obvious enjoyment to the student, and results in an enduring product is simply a privilege and a joy. My goal is to enable students to put their unique stamp on their creations, and I endeavor to bring out the latent talent for design many of us don't know we have within ourselves!

Besides quilting, I enjoy gardening, cooking in general, making jams and baking bread in particular, hiking, kayaking, and traveling. My travels have brought me some opportunities to teach in Singapore and in Australia and put me in contact with many wonderful people in the local quilting communities.

I was born in South Africa and my husband and I came to the United States in 1977. We lived first in Madison, Wisconsin, where I began my quilting pursuits, and now reside in Sudbury, Massachusetts. We have two grown sons and one opportunistic cat who, like all other quilters' cats, seems to think the quilts are made solely with her best interests in mind.

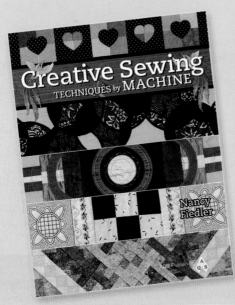

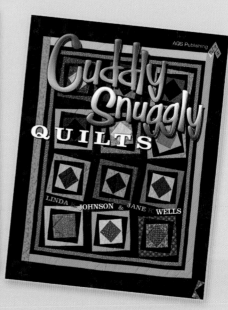

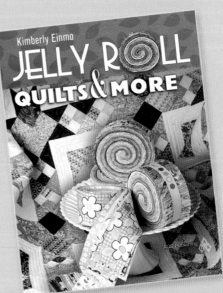